The BHS
Training Manual
FOR
Stage 3 and PTT

The BHS
Training Manual
FOR
Stage 3 and PTT

BRITISH HORSE SOCIETY

Islay Auty FBHS

KENILWORTH PRESS

First published in 2002 by
Kenilworth Press Ltd
Addington
Buckingham
MK18 2JR

British Library Cataloguing in Publication Data
A catalogue record for this book is available from the British Library.

ISBN 0-872119-46-8

Design by Paul Saunders
Layout by Kenilworth Press
Line drawings by Dianne Breeze and Carole Vincer
Line diagrams by Michael J. Stevens

Printed in Great Britain by MPG Books Ltd (www.mpg-books.co.uk)

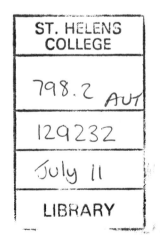

Contents

Picture acknowledgements

All line drawings are by **Dianne Breeze**, with the exception of those on pages 84, 85, 87 and 89, which are by **Carole Vincer**.

The jumping diagrams in section 1.2 are by **Michael J. Stevens**.

Picture sources
The author and publishers wish to acknowledge the following books as sources for some of the illustrations:

- **The BHS Manual of Equitation**, Consultant Editor Islay Auty FBHS, published by Kenilworth Press – pages 20, 22, 41, 97, 109, 171 and 189

- **Threshold Picture Guide No. 43, Functional Anatomy**, by Dr Chris Colles BVetMed, PhD, MRCVS, published by Kenilworth Press – pages 84, 85 and 87

- **Threshold Picture Guide No. 16, Feet and Shoes**, by Toni Webber, published by Kenilworth Press – page 89

- **Teaching Children to Ride**, by Jane Wallace, published by Kenilworth Press – pages 153, 184 and 211

How to Use This Book

THE AIM OF THIS BOOK is to provide students working towards the Stage 3 and/or the Preliminary Teaching Test, with detailed guidance to help prepare thoroughly for the chosen examinations.

The text is clearly divided into sections which fully cover the syllabus and requirements of the Horse Knowledge and Care Stage 3 and Preliminary Teaching Test. In each section the requirements are broken down into bite-size chunks, describing the level of practical and theoretical knowledge expected at this stage. There is also clear indication of how the information is sought from the candidate in the examination situation.

When using this book you can decide to:

- Read it from start to finish, which will give you a very thorough insight into the requirements of the BHS Stage 3 and PTT exams.

- Read each section independently, if for example you have already passed the PTT and need only to study for Stage 3, or vice versa.

- Select whichever section of each exam you particularly want to concentrate on and study that section exclusively.

Ideally this book should be used in conjunction with the following publications:

- The BHS Manual of Equitation

- The BHS Complete Manual of Stable Management

- The BHS Veterinary Manual

These will enhance the information in this book and give you the comprehensive depth of knowledge that should provide the substance to the requirements of the exams.

I make no apology for repeating certain pieces of advice in this book, especially when it comes to practical experience. There is no substitute for 'hands-on' training, and BHS exams at any level are almost impossible to achieve without sufficient practical expertise. **You will not achieve Stage 3/PTT competence purely by reading this book.**

Competence in any vocational occupation can only be achieved through experience – by actually carrying out the necessary tasks for real, in a practical environment and with sufficient regularity. Take every opportunity to work with horses, fulfilling   all the tasks that are compatible with you becoming a competent groom. Make sure that you always adhere to safe practice, with due regard for the welfare of the horse and the safety of yourself and anyone else around. Try to have your practical work regularly supervised so that you do not develop casual or unsafe habits which could 'fail' you in the practical section of an exam: for example, don't leave the horse loose in the stable while you groom him, with the door open and a saddle over the door – for safety, the horse should be tied up, with the door preferably closed and the saddle not in a position where, if pushed off, it could be damaged.

Part 1

Stage 3

Understanding the Stage 3 Exam

YOU MAY HAVE COME TO THE STAGE 3 exam through taking and passing Stage 1 and then Stage 2. If this is the case then you will have already had some experience of the exam situation. You may be coming to the Stage 3 exam as your first BHS exam, because you have accessed this level:

- Through Pony Club 'B' Test achievement.

- Through direct entry resulting from accredited prior learning or experience via an accepted assessment.

- From NVQ.

Whichever the case, preparation is essential. Stage 3 is a big step up from Stage 2, similar to the step between GCSEs at school and then sitting A/S level exams. Achieving Stage 2 means that you are well on the right course towards the next level. It rarely means that you are nearly at Stage 3 level. Allow time and a strategically planned programme of work and learning to aim progressively for the next level of exam. There is no short cut to competence.

The syllabus should be carefully studied and if you are not in a formal training situation, in either a commercial training yard or in an equine college, where the work towards Stage 3 should be planned out for you, then you must work out a programme for yourself. The programme should aim to allow you to cover the areas of the syllabus for which you need further knowledge and training. Time must then be given to allow competence to develop through practice. Learning to 'do' a task once or twice does not convey competence: competence is only achieved through repetition – repetition which should be regularly supervised to make sure that good practice is developed.

The Stage 3 exam is, like all the BHS exams, a very practical exam. Theoretical knowledge is essential as it underpins practical know-how. As discussed elsewhere in this book, knowledge in areas such as the physiology of the horse, endows the person with a greater depth of understanding of the horse's function and therefore will enhance the expertise of caring ability. In all sections of the exam the examiners will be looking for:

- A person with quiet, self-assured confidence.

- A person who is always aware of the horse in a natural caring way (e.g. a gentle pat on the neck or appropriate word when handling the horse).

- A thorough, tidy, workmanlike person (e.g. someone who skips out the stable when working, places tack in a safe position, removes gloves to examine the horse's legs, etc.).

- A person who handles all the horses positively and with firmness.

- A person who offers information concisely and confidently.

One-word answers fail to demonstrate to the examiner that there is a depth of knowledge. Examiners want to pass candidates but they can only assess competence on what they see or hear. At Stage 3 level, the examiner should not have to drag answers from the candidate; the facts should be forthcoming.

Each section of the exam should be explained by the examiner in charge. If at any time you are unsure of what is being asked of you, then you must ask the examiner to clarify either the question or the task that is required.

In any of the riding sections or the lungeing section of the exam, don't be influenced by anyone who tries to tell you about the horse(s). While this might be well intentioned, it is far preferable to take a completely strange horse and assess it for yourself with a 'clean slate' approach. If you listen to snippets of information from well-meaning souls, it is easy to allow these comments to cloud your own judgment of the horse. Advice like 'he doesn't like fillers in the jumps,' might cause you to ride the horse negatively to a filler, expecting him to stop, or perhaps over-ride him for the same reason. If you have no knowledge of the horse then you will ride what you feel, and this is usually the best way. Should the horse then stop you should deal with it as you feel appropriate, whereas if you have prior knowledge of his behaviour it may affect your competence with the horse.

In all situations try to deal with problems as they arise, just as you would at home. If the horse stops at a fence and you feel that the disobedience justifies a smack with the whip, then do so. Good judgment and a positive attitude will be rewarded, especially when it achieves practical results.

Try not to be influenced by how a horse may have gone for another candidate. You will only have seen the horse perform; you will not have felt for yourself how the horse behaved. If you then ride a horse that you have seen behaving badly, you must assess him for yourself and then decide how to deal with it. Do not assume that he will go for you the way he did for someone else, until you have assessed him.

In all the stable management sessions, keep your concentration, listen to the questions and the answer, and make sure that you offer correct information whenever you feel you can.

For the riding and lungeing sessions you should wear smart riding clothes, fawn or light breeches/jodhpurs, long boots, shirt and tie and well fitting jacket (preferably tweed not show navy or black.) Gloves should be worn and a long schooling whip used for the work on the flat and a short whip for the jumping phase. A hat of the correct standard is essential as is a crash helmet for the cross-country phase and a body protector. (For more advice about dress, see sections 1.1.8 and 1.2.8.)

For all the stable management sections, you must be warm and dry, but you must be able to work practically and efficiently around the horses. Breeches and boots would still be correct but if you wish to replace a formal jacket with a tidy sweater (plain blue or black without logos or other patterns) or a plain waistcoat depending on the weather, this would be considered workmanlike. You should keep your hat and gloves with you as these may be needed when trotting the horse up for inspection.

Just as it is important to wear gloves for lungeing or trotting a horse up in hand, it is just as important **NOT** to wear gloves when examining the horse's legs for blemishes or injury.

Avoid jewellery and excessive make-up on an exam day. A hint of make-up is acceptable, but excessive make-up, jewellery or perfume is not appropriate for a practical Stage 3 level groom.

Approach the exam positively. Examiners are not ogres; they recognise that candidates are nervous at the beginning. However, once started the nerves should be dispelled as the competence of the good Stage 3 candidate automatically starts to come through. The greatest satisfaction an examiner can have on any exam day is to pass people because they are well up to the standard required. **Passing people is easy when they are competent and well practised.**

If a pass is not achieved, try to address the weaknesses and, when they have been put right, try again. Examiners do not fail candidates: candidates fail an exam because they are not up to standard, usually in several areas on that day. Candidates do not fail because the horses weren't good enough, because the examiners were miserable or because the centre was horrible: candidates fail because they were not sufficiently competent on the day to demonstrate the standard of work required by the Stage 3 syllabus.

Achieving Stage 3 means that you are a workmanlike rider and competent groom. Competent riders/grooms are much sought after in the equine industry. Achieving Stage 3 gives you a recognised standard of ability in the horse industry.

1.1 Riding on the Flat

1.1.1 Position; aids – application and effect

By the time you have reached this level of training your basic riding position should be established and you should be seeking to develop greater depth and effectiveness through the regular daily riding of as many different horses as possible.

Work without stirrups will help to deepen your seat and develop suppleness, greater feel and coordination of the aids.

You must fully understand the aids you are using to create forward movement through the horse's basic gaits. Through the clear application of a system of aids from seat, legs and hands you should be able to establish communication between yourself and the horse you are riding.

The examiners will be looking for:

- A rider who is secure and balanced in his position on the horse in all three gaits.

- A rider who can show suppleness and ease in his riding.

- A rider who is competent, with and without stirrups, in all paces.

- A rider who can show clear aid application with an effective and harmonious effect on the horse.

- A rider who can carry out ridden exercises accurately, with evidence of preparation for correct execution of the work and an understanding of how to deal with errors and evasions in the horse's way of going.

Correct basic riding position.

- A rider who is capable of riding with confidence in a group of up to five riders in open or closed order.

- A rider who can show competence and confidence on a variety of horses. The rider should be versatile in his ability to motivate the lazier horse while showing tact and harmony with a more sensitive, naturally forward-going horse.

1.1.2 Working the horse in

At Stage 3 level you must show a knowledge of how to 'work the horse in', appropriately and effectively, demonstrating an understanding of the gaits and how they can best be used to loosen the horse, warm him up and supple his muscles, providing a basis from which further work can be developed.

When working a horse in, you must show an understanding of what you are trying to achieve and why you have chosen the work shown. If, for example, the horse is presented 'cold' from the stable, you may need to develop the horse's walk, trot and canter to loosen him up progressively. Sometimes (e.g. on a cold day) it might benefit the horse to trot and canter forward quite positively, to warm him up and prevent him from becoming tense, primarily through feeling cold. On another occasion it might be more appropriate to move around in walk for a time on both reins, before introducing trot or canter. There can be no one single plan that applies to the working in of all horses.

The aims of working in should be to:

- Warm the horse's muscles and systematically loosen him up through progressive work, to prepare for subsequent work.

- Develop controlled forward movement.

- Develop responsiveness and obedience to the aids.

- Establish communication between horse and rider.

- Produce a horse that is mentally and physically ready for further progressive work.

1.1.3 Assessing the horse's way of going

At Stage 3 level you must be able to assess the horse's basic way of going. You should understand the timing and sequence of the horse's basic gaits. Clear knowledge of rhythm, forward movement, balance, speed of the pace (tempo) and elasticity within the gaits should all be evident. You must understand and be able to recognise submission in the horse and the form, or outline, in which the horse works.

In discussing the horse's form, you must be aware of the shape that the horse's body takes, from his croup through to his poll.

The following questions will help identify the criteria which are applicable when assessing the horse's way of going:

- Is the horse mentally and physically tuned in to the rider?

- Is the horse working with rhythm in all three basic gaits?

Horse and rider in balance and harmony. Horse working in a soft, round form, accepting the rider's aids.

Loss of harmony. Horse showing resistance and hollowness; rider showing tension and stiffness in position.

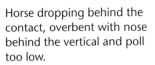

Horse dropping behind the contact, overbent with nose behind the vertical and poll too low.

- Is the horse moving genuinely forward in his work?

- Is the horse developing suppleness and elasticity in his work?

- Can the rider make transitions and changes of direction whilst maintaining balance and submission throughout the work?

- Is the horse's form elastic and flexible, with suppleness through his longitudinal line (from croup to poll) and with a similar elasticity laterally (from side to side)?

- Is the horse attentive and fully obedient to the rider's aids?

Answering the above questions should enable you to consider any horse's way of going and give an assessment of the quality of his work.

1.1.4 Progressing the ridden work

At Stage 3 level you should be capable of working the horse in and then choosing appropriate work to develop the horse further.

Very generally, the horse's work can be developed through the use of transitions to begin to engage the hindquarters and encourage him to take more weight onto the hind legs. Similarly, turns and circles and the development of lateral work will progress the horse's lateral suppleness and elasticity. As a rider, you should be looking for increasing roundness and suppleness in the horse, from which the quality of the gaits will then develop. The horse's range of paces (e.g. his ability to shorten and lengthen his stride within each pace) will increase with correct progressive work.

In the Stage 3 exam you should be capable of showing some of the following work and demonstrating an awareness of what to use and when, with each horse you ride:

- Transitions from one pace to another, or transitions to shorten and lengthen the stride within each pace.

- Progressive transitions from one pace to another and direct transitions (e.g. from walk to canter or trot to halt).

- Development of turns and circles.

- Use of turn on the forehand or turn about the forehand.

- Development of simple lateral work (leg yielding).

1.1.5 Assessing a second or subsequent horse

The criteria in section 1.1.3 apply to the general assessment of any horse. There are some additional considerations that may be useful when riding a horse that has been worked by someone else before you ride it. The horse may have been loosened up or worked in in such a way that he is not relaxed or forward in his way of going. He may be behind the leg and inattentive to the aids in general. He may be tense as a result of unsympathetic or over-demanding riding. Similarly, he may be idle and lacking inspiration through passive or inadequate riding by the previous rider. The rider at Stage 3 level should be able to decide:

- How relaxed the horse is and whether he is in tune with the approach of the rider.

- How responsive he is to the aids.

- How forward and cooperative he is to the work asked of him.

At Stage 3 you must show some ability to adapt your riding to suit the needs of the horse. You should be capable of:

- Choosing work to calm a tense or anxious horse.

- Riding more positively with a horse that is lazy or uncooperative.

- Showing empathy and understanding when the horse starts to improve. Conversely, knowing when to stop expecting more from a horse that is mentally or physically incapable of giving more.

- Praising the horse when the gaits improve or are of a more satisfactory standard in comparison to earlier work.

- Giving the horse a breather or a long rein before over-working him in an effort to further prove your own competence.

- Having sufficient confidence in your own riding to be able to recognise that, from the saddle, what might feel like a disappointing ride may nevertheless be an improvement on how the horse had been going previously.

- Discussing the basic way of going to show an understanding of good and poor quality work.

1.1.6 Talking about the horses you have ridden

When talking about any horse's way of going there are a number of criteria, such as rhythm, forwardness, and acceptance of the aids, which are common to any horse, whether describing an advanced horse, a novice, or a 'green' or untrained horse. It is important, however, that any discussion about a horse does not sound so stereotypical that it could apply to any horse, and is not specific about an individual horse. It is useful to practise talking to someone else about horses you ride, so that it becomes familiar to you to discuss how they have gone.

Discussing a horse's performance should be brief and to the point, covering the main facts, and not ending up with a lengthy description which gives little factual information about the horse. The main criteria to include are:

- Does the horse have three correct basic gaits? A four-time walk, a two-time trot and a three-time canter?

- Does the horse have rhythm in all three gaits?

- Is the horse genuinely forward from the leg and generally accepting the aids?

- Is the horse relaxed in his way of going, or tense and anxious? The latter may adversely affect his way of going, for example, making the steps short and choppy through lack of relaxation.

- Does the horse accept the leg and hand aids?

- Does the horse work in a round frame from active hind legs to a confident connection in the rein?

- Does the horse work 'straight' on straight and curved lines (i.e. do the hind legs follow the track of the front legs)?

- Does the horse give a clear feeling of bending more easily in one direction (soft side or hollow side) in comparison to the other side which is more stiff (the horse showing reluctance to bend through his whole frame on the stiff side)?

- What is the horse's overall attitude to the rider – does he give a feeling of being on the rider's side and wanting to work with him?. Conversely, is the feeling one of anxiety, tension or wilful independence.

- Ultimately, was the horse a pleasure to ride or was he difficult and uncooperative?

1.1.7 Dealing with problems in the ridden work

Riding a horse who feels out of harmony with you is difficult under any circumstances. When this happens during an examination or a competition it can be very disheartening. Naturally you want to produce your best performance – but unfortunately the horse is not aware that an examination day is different to any other day. Often he reacts to the anxiety in the rider and this can adversely affect the results, certainly in the rider's perception. This is where experience is so vital. Training helps to educate the rider in every respect but ultimately your trainer cannot help you in an exam or competition environment. As a prospective Stage 3 candidate it is essential that you learn to deal with problems in any situation and thus develop true ability as an effective rider.

When problems arise some of the following tactics may help you work through to a more satisfactory outcome:

- Try to work the horse in a free space, particularly if he is tense and unpredictable; stay away from other riders so that you have room to work through the problem.

- Be aware of other riders who may be having problems; stay out of their way so that they do not have to worry about your proximity to them. (It may be you next time!)

- If you are losing control then it often helps to come down a pace (if in canter, then trot, if in trot then return to walk).

- Try to avoid getting into a pulling situation with the horse. If a rider pulls when the horse pulls, then the horse will pull back again, and ultimately he will win through strength. Try to give and retake the reins if the horse tempts you to hold on and pull.

- Use a variety of turns and circles depending on the level of the horse's training.

- Move the horse around and keep him busy; this should help to focus his concentration on you, rather than on resisting.

- Try to find the 'key' to the horse, and when some improvement or harmony is achieved then be quick to praise the horse so he knows when he has gone well.

- Try not to doubt your own ability; persevere with variations in the work until you find the 'key' to the horse and then stay with that area of work and develop it further.

1.1.8 What happens in the riding on the flat exam

Generally speaking, examiners are friendly souls; they are professional people who have two main aims:

- To enjoy passing candidates who are at the standard of exam being taken.

- To maintain and safeguard the standard of each exam by being true to the requirements of the syllabus of each standard.

The following points may help you to give your best on the day:

Planning the day

- Having made the entry for the date required, make sure that you have received a letter of confirmation from the examinations office (the address is given at the back of the book).

- Take the letter with you (it is very unlikely that you will need it but it will have the address of the examination centre on it).

- Make sure that you know where the venue is and how long it takes to get there from your home.

- Allow plenty of time for the journey (to cope with possible breakdowns, heavy traffic, etc.).

- Make a checklist of all the equipment needed for the day. This must include a body protector of the current standard (for cross country) and an approved riding hat.

- Take drinks (according to summer or winter) and some food in case there is nowhere close to have a snack at lunchtime.

- A change of clothes is useful if the weather is bad. This will save you having to spend the afternoon in clothes that got soaked in the morning.

- Take a pair of wellingtons to walk the cross-country course so that your riding boots stay clean for the work on the flat.

On arrival

Try to arrive at the exam centre by 8 am at the latest. Once there, find whoever is in charge of meeting candidates. There should be a list of candidates posted up somewhere, and at least one programme of the day's exam available.

- Make sure your name is on the list and check what number you are. (Occasionally the chief examiner announces the numbers at the initial briefing.)

- There may be instructions for candidates; if not, then ask if it is possible to walk the show-jumping and cross-country courses.

- Assemble in the room allocated for candidates.

- If there is time, walk around the stable yard, especially if it is a centre you have never been to before.

- Make sure you know where the toilets are.

- Leave valuables in your car, but find somewhere safe (you will be allocated somewhere appropriate) to put extra coats, raincoats, back protectors, etc.

- Throughout the day, candidates will be divided into groups usually of between four and six, with one examiner. A second examiner may also be present as a 'probationer' gaining experience. In addition there will be a chief examiner who will move around the groups through the day, overseeing the standard of each candidate. Do not feel intimidated by the presence of the chief examiner; he or she is there to add a balanced opinion having observed the candidate in each section of the exam.

- Riding on the flat is almost always carried out in the morning. Depending on the programme used (see Appendix) the riding on the flat section may interchange with stable management questioning in theory, practical or practical oral sessions.

What to wear for the ridden work

For the riding on the flat, clean beige or fawn breeches/jodhpurs are advisable. White, while acceptable for competition, is not really appropriate for a practical 'working' exam; and coloured breeches may be considered a little casual.

- A jacket should be worn. A tweed-type one is most appropriate; navy or black jackets are perhaps a little too formal.

- Boots should ideally be knee length and must be clean.

- It is professional to wear gloves.

Procedure

The riding on the flat will run as follows:

- There will be up to five riders in a group. The group will receive general directives from a commander on how to progress their work, but they will not actually be told what work to do when.

- The riders will be expected to loosen up the first horse to achieve the best level of work that he might be capable of. They will have about 20 minutes on the first horse.

- During the riding of the first horse the examiner(s) **MAY** ask the rider how the horse feels and what else they want to do to further the work.

- At the end of riding the first horses, the riding examiner, and perhaps the chief examiner, may ask the riders how they feel the work is progressing.

- The riders will then change horses and ride a second horse for about 20 minutes. The examiner(s) will again speak to each rider about how he found the horse.

- The riders are not commanded through this section, other than to guide them generally in the type of work they should be showing. (See current *Examinations Handbook,* available from the BHS Bookshop.)

- The rider chooses the work he feels is appropriate, having assessed the horse himself for a few minutes.

- The rider should be capable of showing transitions between the paces and some shortening or lengthening of stride within the gaits.

- The rider should be able to ride a turn on the forehand or turn about the forehand.

- The rider should be able to show leg yielding and a few steps of rein-back.

- All basic school figures and movements such as turns circles, loops and serpentines should be familiar to the rider.

1.1.9 How to prepare for the riding on the flat exam

It is most important that you work towards a specific exam with a clear idea of the requirements of the syllabus. By Stage 3 level you should already be committed to the horse industry. You may already be working in an establishment where you can gain further tuition towards the next level of exam. It is also of paramount importance that you have achieved the level of competence through genuine practice within the industry. Training is essential. It may be helpful to train with someone who is an examiner (preferably a chief examiner) for BHS Stage 3 and PTT. It may be useful to have a few lessons at the centre where you have chosen to do the exam. This may help to make you more familiar with the surroundings.

Allow yourself a realistic period of time between taking Stage 2 and attempting Stage 3. Do not assume that by passing Stage 2 you can automatically move swiftly on to Stage 3. Instead you need to put yourself on a path towards building your experience and ability to match the Stage 3 requirements. Of course, every person is different, but a **minimum** of six months between Stage 2 and 3 would be appropriate – but only if you are an experienced rider with enough maturity to apply yourself to the study of the practical and theoretical knowledge that Stage 3 will demand.

There is no substitute for practical experience. Formal training will help to guide you towards competence in the exam by presenting the theoretical information in a structured way which you then must learn. Supervised practical sessions on such subjects as the 'hands-on' stable management tasks which will be examined, and lungeing, are also essential.

As a prospective Stage 3 candidate your must take responsibility for making sure that:

- You have ridden as many different horses as possible.

- You have lunged horses regularly for genuine exercise, not just under training or supervision.

- If possible, you have ridden horses in competition, at however basic a level this might be.

- You have some experience of riding in at a competition – working in for show jumping, a dressage test or a clear-round show-jumping track will provide valuable experience which cannot be simulated in any other way.

- Even though it may not have been possible for you to compete, you have taken the trouble to attend competitions, perhaps to help or groom for a friend, or just to observe.

- You have some practical experience of caring for horses during and after competition, and of travelling horses.

A potential employer should feel confident that you, as a holder of the BHS Stage 3 Riding and Horse Knowledge and Care certificate, are:

- Capable of looking after a number of horses, including fit competition horses, school horses, and ponies kept in or out.

- Able to ride any of these horses, maintaining their level of work.

- Capable of being left in sole charge of these horses, on a day-to-day basis, and able to take full care of their needs.

1.2 Jumping

1.2.1 Position; aids – application and effect

At this level you should already have a secure basic jumping position. You should be able to ride with or without stirrups, with a secure lower leg, giving the horse an independent hand which is able to follow the horse's movement fluently in the air over a jump. A secure lower leg should enable you to vary your weight in the saddle and maintain balance with the horse according to his way of going. Generally a light seat position between fences would be expected. There may be times when the rider's position is a little more upright with more weight in the saddle, and other times when the seat is very light with more of the rider's weight in the lower leg and stirrup. There should always be a balance between the weight distribution in these two areas. At no time should one hundred per cent of the rider's weight be either all in the seat or all in the stirrup; there should always be a sliding scale of balance between the two, e.g. 40% in the seat, 60% in the leg or, at another time, perhaps 50% in each.

At Stage 3 the examiner will be looking for:

- A consistency in the rider's position which demonstrates security.

- A rider who is consistently in balance with the horse – this is the most important criterion.

- An ability, because of a good secure position, to control the pace of the horse when jumping.

- A demonstration of an awareness of correct speed when jumping.

- An ability to balance the horse between jumps and to present the horse at the fence in the best way possible to enable the horse to jump.

- An understanding of pace, control, straightness of approach and the ability to ride a good departure from the fence.

- A positive, confident approach to jumping show jumps and cross-country fences.

- An ability to deal with problems which may arise, e.g. a horse running out or refusing to jump.

1.2 2 Working the horse in and starting to jump a grid

Just as for any jumping session, you will need to warm up the horse before you start to jump. You will need to shorten your stirrups to adopt a balanced and secure jumping position, and to check that the girth is firm before you start to jump.

The basic working in of the jumping horse is very similar to that for riding on the flat. The horse must be forward, relaxed, straight and obedient. In fact, all the criteria already discussed apply. In addition to this general warm-up, the following work is specifically directed towards the needs of the jumping horse:

- Acute transitions, such as walk to canter and halt to trot, will help improve the obedience of the jumping horse.

- The ability to shorten and lengthen the canter is vital, as much of a jumping track will be ridden in canter.

- The ability to maintain canter around a corner will help to ensure that the horse is able to ride a corner 'on the aids' and be ready to jump a fence which may be on a diagonal out of the corner.

- Sometimes the use of rein-back as a working-in exercise will engage the hindquarters more. The engagement of the hindquarters is essential to the efficiency of the jumping horse.

- Accuracy of lines and control of the horse's shoulders and hindquarters on straight lines and curves is also vital for the show-jumping rider.

Once the horse is well warmed up, jumping can commence. The warm-up session progresses through gridwork, then the jumping sequence is typically as follows:

- The **first fence** is a cross-pole (with or without a trot placing pole), which may be approached from a straight line out of trot. A placing pole would assist in positioning the horse's point of take-off. The distance should be 8ft or 9ft (2.4–2.7m) from the placing pole to the cross-pole, and the latter should not be too steep sided, which would make the fence very narrow at the point where the horse would actually jump.

- When the horse negotiates this first element confidently then a **second fence** may be erected at approximately 18ft (5.4m) from the first cross-pole. This would enable the horse to approach in trot, jump the first element, take one non-jumping stride and then jump the second fence, landing in canter for a straight line of departure.

- The second fence would probably be a small vertical fence.

- When the horse moves fluently and calmly through this simple layout, then a **third fence** would be introduced. It is optional whether the third fence is placed at one non-jumping stride away or two non-jumping strides from the previous element.

- One non-jumping stride would require a distance of about 21ft (6.3m), whereas two non-jumping strides would dictate a distance of about 30ft (9m).

- The third jump could be a small, ascending spread fence or another vertical.

- The height of the fences would depend on the level of competence of both horse and rider. In a Stage 3 training session and in a grid which is used for a Stage 3 exam, the fences usefully could be between 2ft 9in and 3ft (85–90cm).

The object of building up the horse's work through a grid is:

- It assists the rider's confidence because he does not need to worry about where the horse might take off for the fence because the measured distance dictates an optimum point of take-off.

- It develops the horse's confidence and is especially helpful for young or uneducated horses and for less experienced riders.

TYPICAL GRID

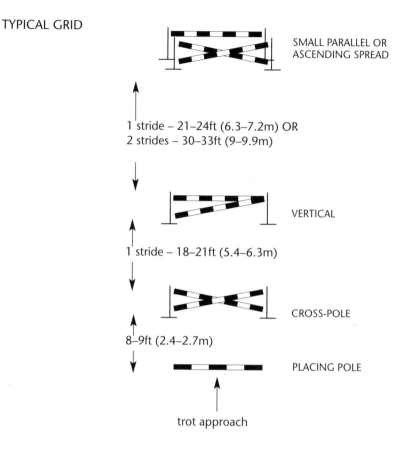

SMALL PARALLEL OR
ASCENDING SPREAD

1 stride – 21–24ft (6.3–7.2m) OR
2 strides – 30–33ft (9–9.9m)

VERTICAL

1 stride – 18–21ft (5.4–6.3m)

CROSS-POLE

8–9ft (2.4–2.7m)

PLACING POLE

trot approach

- It helps to teach the rider to judge pace and distances for himself.

- It helps teach the horse to develop adaptability in his stride.

- It enables the rider to concentrate more closely on maintaining his balance and position and feel through the jumps.

1.2.3 Developing the grid into a course of show jumps

Working a horse and rider through a grid gets the partnership thinking forward and helps develop a confident and working relationship between the two.

SUGGESTED STAGE 3
COURSE PLANS

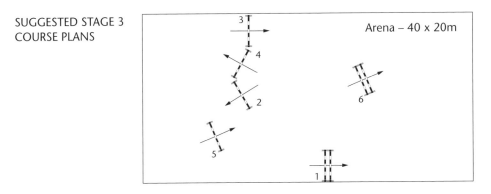

Arena – 40 x 20m

NOTES
- Feet interlocked on fences 2, 3 and 4.
- Fences 5–6 related distance
- RH wing of fence 5 in line with LH wing of fence 1

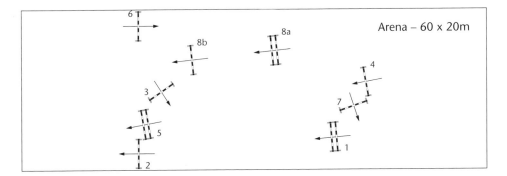

Arena – 60 x 20m

NOTES
- LH wing fence 1 is 2m in from outside wall
- Fence 2 minimum of 15m (50ft) from end of school
- Fences 2 and 5 and 4 and 7, wings interlocked
- Double is kinder on candidates if 2 strides, with upright coming out
- Fences 4–5 related distance

Gridwork is an active part of warming up the horse for more serious jump-ing perhaps later (e.g. a course or bigger, plain fences). It is then easy to develop a course of fences using the grid, or part of it, as an integral part of a course.

If the work has developed from a trot approach (as described) then the horse

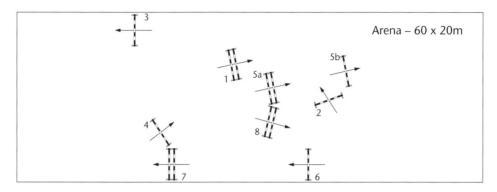

NOTES
- Put diagonal fences in first when building
- 4–5a related distance (4,5 strides)
- 6–7 related distance (4,5 strides)
- No fence closer than 15m (50ft) from end of school
- RH wing of fence 1 in line with LH wing of fence 5a
- Wings 5a and 8 interlocked, as fences 4 and 7

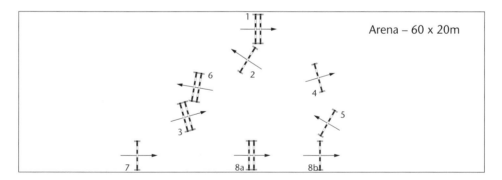

NOTES
- Fence 7–8a, 3 strides
- 8a–8b, 1 stride
- 5–6 related distance, 4/5 strides
- 3–4 related distance, 5 strides

and rider need to jump one or two fences from canter before riding a course in entirety. Alternatively the rider might start his course with the grid (with a trot approach) and then depart in canter from the grid and flow on into a course of jumps (depending on how the course is set).

The grid (or part of it) can be left in the course, if appropriate, to utilise the jump(s). If sited half way around a course, then it would be most useful to use the second and third elements of the grid to form a double within the course. If used as a double, the distance of 21ft (6.3m) might need to be lengthened a little to nearer 24ft (7.2m) – although in an indoor (or outdoor) school, where the surface may make the distances ride a little short, it might be wiser to keep the distances on the shorter side. It is preferable to encourage horses to shorten their stride, thus making the jump rounder and more athletic, rather than have distances which are long and encourage a horse to flatten and hollow his jump.

The course of show jumps will be between 3ft (90cm) and 3ft 3in. (100cm) high and should be progressive (e.g. a small inviting fence at first, building up to more difficult fences throughout the course).

At Stage 3 you should be able to walk a show-jumping course and then ride it showing the following:

- You must be able to ride a fluent round, showing judgment of pace and the ability to balance the horse between jumps.

- You must show how to ride a good track between fences, using the area to balance the horse, change canter leads if and where appropriate and present the horse straight in front of each jump with sufficient energy to negotiate the jump.

- You must understand why problems arise (e.g. stops or run-outs) and show an ability to deal with these problems, producing a favourable outcome if possible.

- You must demonstrate a well-balanced, secure position both on the flat between jumps and in the air.

- You must demonstrate confidence and practical ability.

1.2.4 Dealing with jumping problems

Horses are not naturally jumping animals – if they were we would never be able to contain them in fields with fences of around four foot. They jump through generosity and training.

When problems arise it is usually due to a lack of training or a flaw in the training system. It may also be due to poor riding, which causes the horse to lose confidence and then stop jumping. Problems in a jumping horse tend to be more highlighted than those in a dressage horse, for the simple reason that if a show jumper stops jumping or knocks fences down it is very evident!

Here we will deal with minor problems that might arise when taking a Stage 3 exam and jumping an unfamiliar horse around a course of show jumps for the first time.

If the horse has gone badly for another rider before you, the problem may be exacerbated. However, the examiner will be sympathetic to any problems that you inherit in this way.

When figuring out why a horse is showing problems in its jumping try to work systematically.

- Is the horse rhythmical and balanced in its trot and canter (when not jumping)?

- Does the horse become tense and anxious and change his basic way of going as soon as he is shown a jump?

- Does the horse stay straight in the approach to the jumps?

- Does the horse run away from the jump with little control?

- Does the horse draw back and seem reluctant to approach a jump confidently?

- Does the horse consistently knock fences down, stop or run out?

In dealing with the problem, the most useful advice is:

- Try to establish and maintain a controlled, rhythmical approach.

- If necessary, make an approach from a half circle, or a shorter line of approach.

- Perhaps make the approach from trot rather than from canter to improve the control.

- Be positive in giving the horse confidence with an active leg to the fence, a short enough rein to control lack of straightness but a light seat and a quickly allowing hand when he commits himself to jump.

- Be quick to reward the horse when he is obedient so that he gains confidence in his success.

- A short, sharp reminder with a whip, if justified, is quite acceptable, particularly if the horse responds positively.

1.2.5 Riding a second horse

Your second horse in the jumping section of the Stage 3 exam will usually be for cross-country riding. Most of the points referring to jumping in general apply here also. It is essential that the rider shows a secure and confident position across country. The rider must choose the pace according to the going on the course. If it is very slippery or wet then judgment must be used with regard to pace and where a slower speed would be more appropriate. You should work in the horse for your own benefit, but understanding that the horse is already warm and has previously jumped.

Some of the problems described above may relate to a horse that has been ridden passively or inadequately and has taken advantage of the rider. In this case positive riding would be necessary. It would also be advisable to 'open the horse up' a little (towards gallop), but make sure that you are in control when you increase the pace.

1.2.6 Developing cross-country riding and jumping

As with the riding on the flat, expertise in jumping, whether show jumping or across country, is developed by riding as many different horses as possible both under instruction and in practice. The next best thing to actually riding is to watch other good riders and learn from their techniques.

At Stage 3 you should be capable of:

- Judging speed and balance between fences and in the approach to a fence.

- Considering the effect of the ground on how the horse might perform, e.g. hard ground may make the horse cautious and reluctant to jump boldly; heavy ground may slow the horse and reduce energy.

- Knowing the effect of gradients (uphill or downhill) on the balance and ability of the horse to jump.

- Knowing that island fences may need more accuracy in riding than jumps enclosed in a fence line.

- Knowing the effect of bright sunlight and dark shaded areas on the horse's ability to judge points of take-off.

- Understanding how to ride into and out of water, jump ditches, angled fences and simple combination jumps.

In preparation for Stage 3 you can build confidence and expertise by riding out

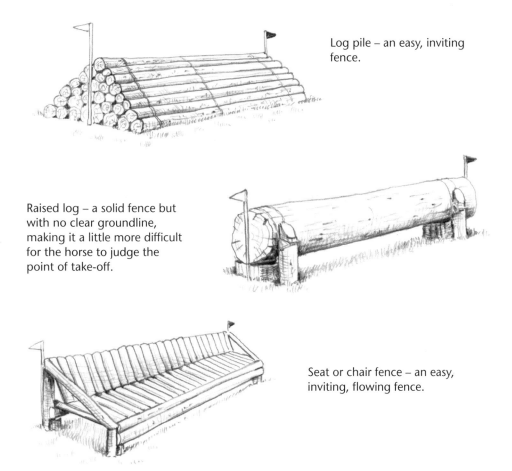

Log pile – an easy, inviting fence.

Raised log – a solid fence but with no clear groundline, making it a little more difficult for the horse to judge the point of take-off.

Seat or chair fence – an easy, inviting, flowing fence.

in open country whenever possible. Cross-country competitions, hunter trials and schooling over cross-country fences will all help to develop competence. Pony Club, Riding Club and British Eventing competitions are ideal environments in which to develop cross-country skills.

1.2.7 Assessing the jumping horse's way of going and being able to discuss it

All the criteria described in section 1.1.6 apply here when discussing the way of going of a jumping horse. Additional criteria for consideration are:

■ Does the horse 'take on' the fence? As he approaches the fence is he enthusiastic and moving confidently to the fence while keeping the same rhythm, or does he take control and dictate the speed and approach with little influence from his rider?

■ Does the horse draw back on the approach to the fence, making the rider work harder to keep the same impulsion before the jump?

■ Does the horse maintain a straight line of approach or does he deviate and jump to the side of the fence?

■ If the horse jumps crookedly, is it always to the same direction – i.e. does he jump to the left or the right consistently?

■ Does the horse give a comfortable, 'round' feel in the air, with the neck forward and stretched out in front of the rider, or does the horse's head come up and the back become very hollow?

■ Does the horse land in balance and move away from the fence in a good rhythmical canter, or does it take time to re-establish control and balance on the departure from the jump?

■ Does the horse become increasingly excited the more he jumps, with a relative loss of control from the rider?

■ Does the horse start to make mistakes as he becomes more tense and out of control?

When talking about any horse try to establish a clear plan of what there is to say. It is important to convey facts about the horse and not end up waffling, with no clear information forthcoming, or talking so generally that what is said does not really apply to the horse you have ridden.

With regard to the jumping horse try to impart the following information:

- Describe the horse's basic paces, particularly the canter, which is the most important pace for the jumping horse.

- Describe the canter in terms of rhythm, forwardness, 'jump' or athleticism off the ground, and the horse's ability to move up to bigger strides and then collect into rounder, shorter, more powerful, contained strides.

- Describe the control and attitude of the horse when moving towards and away from a fence.

- Describe how you think you may be able to adjust the pace to be able to turn corners and shorten and lengthen strides between fences.

- Describe your overall control and harmony with the horse.

- If you feel that you cannot stop or turn, then say so! It will not necessarily reflect on your ability to ride that particular horse.

- Once you have jumped the horse, describe the feeling the horse gives you when he jumps (e.g. scopey, limited, hollow, etc.).

1.2.8 What happens in the jumping exam

In the Stage 3 exam, you will ride in a group of up to five riders.

You will each ride one horse over a course of show jumps, and one horse around a number of cross-country fences.

The show jumps may be up to 3ft 3in. (100cm), and the cross-country fences will be up to 3ft (90cm). Both courses should be built, flagged and numbered on your arrival at the exam centre. It is advisable to walk both courses thoroughly before the briefing for the exam day. Make sure that you allow plenty of time when you arrive to do this (up to half an hour), and bring a pair of wellingtons so that you can keep your boots clean for the riding sections of the exam.

The show-jumping section will run as follows:

- The riders should all be riding with their stirrups at jumping length and will have checked their girth prior to jumping.

- A grid will then be built up as described in section 1.2.2 and 1.2.3, and the riders, having warmed up in walk, trot and canter, will be invited to start jumping the grid.

- It is important that you always approach the grid in a space well away from other riders and in a position to circle away easily if a fence should be knocked down and need rebuilding.

- Each rider should approach the grid on his own terms, i.e. when the grid is clear and the previous rider has jumped the last element.

- Each rider should be able to jump the grid at least twice and be aiming to find the best balance and approach for his horse.

- Each rider must show judgment for increasing or decreasing energy in the approach as they feel appropriate.

- When the grid has been developed to three elements and jumped to the satisfaction of the examiners by all the candidates, then the grid, or part of it, will be incorporated into a course.

- Each rider in turn will then be asked to jump the show-jumping course on the horse that they have worked through the grid.

- The show-jumping course is a schooling round. The examiners are looking for the rider's ability to deal with problems as they arise. A clear round is desirable but not essential. Faults are judged on how they are dealt with rather than how many you accumulate.

- Even if the rider is unfortunate enough to fall off, this does not constitute a failure of the standard aimed for. How the rider deals with the incident is much more relevant.

Having completed your show-jumping round, you will then change horses to prepare for the cross-country section. A period of working in, as for the show jumping, will allow you to familiarise yourself with the new horse. One or two practice fences may be jumped – these may be natural obstacles, such as a log if available; otherwise the rider will work in over a show jump. The riders will then be asked to jump the cross-country fences, usually going in numerical order.

As a Stage 3 rider you should be showing:

- A balanced, secure position.

- The ability to ride purposefully across country at a good pace, using judgment as to the ground conditions.

- The ability to deal with any evasions (stops or run-outs) as they arise.

- The ability to negotiate a short course of varied cross-country type fences in good style and control.

1.2.9 How to prepare for the jumping exam

Here again there is no substitute for practice. You should try to ride a variety of horses in different jumping situations as often as you can. Whilst training is essential to develop a secure, effective jumping position, you must have the opportunity to develop that position through practice. Riding in any form of competition will be beneficial, as will assisting more competent riders in the competition environment, so that learning is achieved through observation.

It is helpful to have your progress assessed by a trainer who is also a BHS examiner (preferably a chief examiner). Do be honest with yourself and take their advice if they tell you that you are not quite ready for the exam. It is preferable to be well up to the standard or even a little above it before present-ing yourself for the exam. Exams put stress on everyone, and stress may reduce your normal standard of competence. You must take this into account and make sure that you are ready to pass on your first attempt, by being well up to standard.

1.3 Horse Knowledge and Care – Theory

THIS SECTION CONSISTS of a session of oral questioning, usually in a lecture room or similar. You will be part of a group of up to six candidates. Your group will often be asked to sit in numerical order, with one examiner asking the questions.

A question will often be directed at one person initially, to begin the answer, then opportunity will be given to other candidates to add information or to disagree with what has been said.

It is important not to talk over another candidate, but also not to lose the chance to offer information on as many subjects as possible, to show your knowledge. While the examiner should draw information equally from all candidates, inevitably the more forthcoming individuals will always be ready to volunteer plenty of answers. Ultimately candidates are passed (or failed) on the facts (or lack of them) that are given during the session. It is up to each candidate to offer as much knowledge as possible on all subjects. If the examiner constantly asks you to stop when you feel you are giving plenty of answers, do not be put off, as this usually means that the examiner is content with your knowledge and wants to draw out other people who are saying less.

1.3.1 Daily routine

As a holder of Stage 3 Horse Knowledge and Care, or The Groom's Certificate, you should be totally competent to take charge of the welfare of a number of horses, both stabled and at grass. It will therefore be necessary for you to show a thorough understanding of daily routine in a stable yard and how to organise it.

■ The candidate must be able to explain the planning of the day when caring for up to four horses, stabled or at grass.

■ The need for a daily routine and a suggestion of how a day may be planned may be asked.

■ The organisation of early morning stables, including initial checks, mucking out, feeding, quartering and supervision of any 'out' horses/ponies may be discussed.

■ The planning of exercise, discussing the reasons for lungeing, hacking, or riding and leading for exercise as an alternative to schooling.

■ The advantages and disadvantages of turning out horses that are in work on a daily or regular basis.

■ The benefits of when and how to groom stabled horses.

■ The supervision of 'out' horses/ponies, including knowledge of when these should be brought in for work and under what conditions.

■ Feeding plan for the day, to include stabled and horses at grass.

■ Additional stable duties that may be integrated into the daily routine, including care and maintenance of tack and equipment, yard organisation such as care of muck heap, feed room, tack room and other communal working areas.

■ Afternoon and evening stables, including the importance of late-night checks.

■ There must be a practical and realistic understanding of the timescale of certain stable-yard tasks (e.g. a competent Stage 3 holder should be capable of mucking out and completing early morning duties for four stabled horses in approximately one hour).

1.3.2 Feeding

Feeding is a very important subject with regard to the care and management of horses. Poor understanding of feeding, or poor practice, can cause major problems in the horse, some of which can occur quite suddenly and may have devastating effects.

Here are a few:

- The horse develops digestive problems as a result of incorrect feeding.

- The horse loses weight and lacks energy for the work required of him.

- The horse gains weight and becomes unruly, difficult to manage in the stable and badly behaved when ridden.

- The horse may suffer bodily, e.g. tack which fails to fit if a horse has lost weight for any reason may cause injury, or leg injuries may occur due to being overweight.

- The horse may develop skin problems as a result of over-rich food.

- The horse may develop a fluid build-up in his lower limbs ('filled legs') due to excess food.

As a Stage 3 candidate you will be expected to understand:

- The nutrients which make up the horse's diet and the role they play (e.g. protein is for growth and repair of tissue).

- The basic importance of all the nutrients, including the value of vitamins, minerals and water in the horse's diet.

- The difference between forage (hay, haylage) and concentrates and their roles and ratio in different horses' diets.

- The value of grass or other green food in the diet.

- The range of different feeds available currently for horses and their relative advantages and disadvantages.

The organisation of a feed room or feed store will be discussed (see also section 1.3.6) and you should have a clear understanding of:

- The relative size for a number of horses.

- The type of storage containers.

- The lighting and ideal power facilities.

- Additional features which might be of help or relevant (e.g. a weigh scale).

- How to plan feedcharts for a variety of horses in different types of work (e.g. young horses, ponies, horses in medium work, ill horses, etc.).

You must show an understanding of feeding a range of different types of foodstuffs. You should have ideas about the advantages and disadvantages of feeding compound mixes or cubes compared to more traditional 'straight' components of feeds (e.g. oats or barley). You should also know how to prepare feeds such as:

- Cooked linseed/barley.

- Sugarbeet.

- A bran mash (and how to use it).

- Soaked or steamed hay.

It is always preferable that a candidate can speak from practical, first-hand experience of horses they have fed on a regular basis – horses for which they have had responsibility. This practical knowledge, however, must be supported by a sound understanding of the theory of feeding. You will be expected to be confident about discussing the amounts of feed you would give to various working horses. In discussing feeds you should feel secure about discussing the ratio of forage/fibre to concentrate in the horse's diet .

1.3.3 Fitness

A state of fitness can be defined as the horse's ability to carry out the work asked of him easily and with no ill-effects during the work, as a direct result of the work itself, or afterwards. At Stage 3 level you must understand the basic principles by which the horse's fitness is developed. You must be able to recognise how fit a horse might be and describe how you might find out the level of fitness by simple means such as:

- How easily the horse works.

- How much he sweats when working.

- How much he blows when working.

- How tired he seems after work.

- How quickly he recovers his normal breathing and behaviour.

- The horse's physical appearance (how much weight he is carrying and muscle development).

There must be appreciation of how progressive work builds up fitness levels, and an understanding that different types and breeds of horses will take varying lengths of time to achieve fitness. At Stage 3 you will be expected to know:

- Approximately how long it would take to get a horse fit for Riding Club or Pony Club type events, or for basic endurance type rides of up to 25 miles.

- What factors might affect the progression of a fittening programme, e.g. weather conditions, injury, how long the horse has been out of work.

- What work might be appropriate in the first four weeks of fittening.

- What work might be included in the next four-week period.

- How canter work would be introduced.

- How the canter work would be further developed to benefit the horse's fitness regime.

- What problems within the fitness programme might alter or affect progress (e.g. unexpected injury).

You should have knowledge of how different types of work are used to develop the horse's fitness, and be able to discuss the relative values of:

- Walking exercise.

- Developing trot work.

- Hill work.

- Canter work.

- Developing canter into short gallops.

- Lungeing.

Knowledge of preparing horses for shows and competitions may be requested. Sometimes this information can be included in the discussion on daily routine, as a Stage 3 candidate should be able to plan a day which includes preparing horses for competition.

The following information could be sought:

- How much time should you allow for plaiting a horse's mane? Tail? (Sewn, or secured with rubber bands?)

- How long should you allow for a journey? (You would be advised of distance.)

- What travel arrangements might be made (e.g.rugs, protective clothing, hay for the journey)?

- How would you deal with horses immediately after competition (e.g. after a cross-country round)? (See also section 1.4.7.)

- How would you prepare for travelling home?

- How would you deal with horses on their return and/or on the day after a competition.

> **Note that section 1.3.4 may be covered in the Practical or Practical Oral section of the Stage 3 Horse Knowledge and Care examination**

1.3.4 Preparation for shows and competitions

This will cover aspects of preparing horses for competitive outings. You will be expected to understand the following:

- How to plan a schedule to allow adequate time to prepare one or more horses, including travelling time to the competition.

- How to estimate the time it might take you to groom, plait, and prepare for the journey.

- How to take into account the approximate length of the journey.

You may be asked:

- What equipment would you take with you in the lorry?

- What provision do you need to make for the horses' comfort at a show? (For example, water, feed, hay, etc.)

- What equipment may be necessary for the competition? (For example, studs, spare reins, girth, specialist boots or bandages, etc.)

- What additional equipment might it be wise to include? (For example, tools to remove a shoe, grooming kit, washing down equipment, etc.)

There may be discussion on such topics as:

- When to plait.

- When to use rubber bands and when to sew.

- Whether to travel the horse with or without a haynet.

- How much water to allow him during a competition day.

Try to remember that some questions do not necessarily have a 'right' or 'wrong' answer. If you can speak from some personal practical experience then this is always preferable. For example, you may have travelled a particular horse with a haynet because he travels more quietly and the food keeps him more settled. However, if a horse is going to be involved in strenuous exercise immediately on arrival at the venue, then it may be preferable to travel him without hay. Neither answer is 'right' or 'wrong' at the expense of the other.

There may be some questions on clipping with regard to preparing horses for competition. These may relate to:

- Why you might choose a full clip for a horse competing.

- Why you might trace or blanket clip a competition horse.

You should feel sufficiently confident about preparing horses for competition that you could:

- Plan the day for two horses to go to a competition and two to stay at home.

- Include a plan of how long you would allow to prepare each horse and a morning plan of estimated time for departure, taking into account preparing both horses and leaving the two remaining at home well provided for.

- Estimate a designated journey (e.g. for 50 miles, in a lorry, allow two hours).

- Demonstrate that you are sufficiently organised in your thinking and management of the day, that nothing essential would be forgotten.

> Note that section 1.3.5 may also be covered in the Practical or Practical Oral section of the Stage 3 Horse Knowledge and Care examination

1.3.5 Illness and lameness, and their management

All horses, unfortunately, are subject to illnesses and lameness. Well-managed horses are less susceptible to problems than those which are not well cared for, but nevertheless awareness of common illnesses and lameness is essential for the competent Stage 3 person. The **BHS Veterinary Manual** by P. Stewart Hastie provides comprehensive information on many common ailments suffered by horses and is well worth studying.

When it comes to recognising illness or lameness the first consideration must be an awareness that something is abnormal. Good knowledge of the horse will help, but the competent groom will be capable of spotting the early signs of ill-health or lameness even in a horse they are not familiar with.

The competent Stage 3 candidate should be able to prioritise the following:

- Signs of good health (e.g. eating, drinking, healthy eyes, skin, behaviour).

- Willingness to work and regular gaits.

- No change or reduction in performance.

- No physical signs to give early warning of a problem.

Having recognised signs of illness or lameness the next decision must be whether or not to call the vet. This decision may not ultimately be within the remit of the Stage 3 holder, but there may be an occasion, in an emergency, when you may need to take the initiative.

The decision as to whether to call the vet may be influenced by any of the following:

- Is the horse running a high temperature (2° above normal) with accompanying signs of illness (e.g. tucked up, staring coat, looking unhappy, off food)?

- Have the symptoms come on quite acutely (in a few hours or overnight)?

- Does the horse show signs of gut pain (pawing, getting up and down, rolling)?

- Is there an acute injury with an open wound which is either bleeding profusely or obviously needs stitching?

- Is there acute lameness, with the horse showing reluctance to put weight on the injured leg/foot?

- If you have attempted to monitor and treat the horse yourself over a few hours, have the symptoms abated or got worse?

- If in **ANY** doubt at all, particularly if the horse does not belong to you, **CALL THE VET**.

Lameness and foot problems

Recognising lameness should be a simple case of noting which of the four legs is not carrying the same weight as the others. When a horse is sound, all four legs bear weight evenly in the rhythm of the gait and the gait therefore looks regular. If one leg is in any way damaged, the injured leg will not take its share of the horse's weight, and this is symptomised by an irregular gait.

Isolating the lame leg is relatively straightforward. In watching the front action of the horse, the head nods lower as the sound leg comes to the ground and takes extra weight. From behind, the horse's hip will lower on the sound side, again as the horse takes the extra weight onto the good leg. Having isolated the lame leg, it may then be more difficult to find the exact area of injury, and this may be where the vet or farrier's expertise will be called upon.

A large percentage of lameness originates from problems in the foot, so this would usually be the first area of investigation. When checking the feet the following points might assist in identifying the source of the lameness:

- Any obvious displacement of a shoe with a nail apparently penetrating the foot.

- Any obstacle, such as a sharp stone, wedged into the foot or under any part of the shoe.

- Heat in the foot (the outer wall or undersole feeling much hotter when compared with the other foot).

- Tenderness or flinching when the foot (wall or sole) is tapped with a hoof pick or small hammer.

- Obvious reluctance to put the foot on the floor and bear weight (this could come from injury higher up the leg).

When checking for lameness it is much easier if someone else can run the horse up in hand so that the walk and trot can be observed from in front, from the side, and from behind. If, however, you are alone, then you must trot the horse on a hard surface and 'listen' to the regularity of the footfall. The degree of lameness may differ depending on whether the surface is hard or soft. Usually if a horse is more lame on hard ground the type of lameness is likely to be associated with a 'bony' problem, e.g. the formation of a splint, which would be made more painful through the concussion of hard ground. A horse which is more lame on soft ground is more likely to be suffering a soft tissue injury (e.g. in a muscle or tendon) which pulls more in soft ground.

The following lameness and foot ailments should be understood:

- Nail prick and nail bind

- Seedy toe

- Sandcracks

- Quittor

- Navicular-type syndrome

- Laminitis

- Ringbone and sidebone

- Corns

- Bruised sole

- Puncture wounds in the foot

- Thrush

General conditions

With an illness such as a cold, or one or two of the more obscure but nevertheless serious infections such as 'strangles' or equine influenza, the horse will be very off-colour. The following illnesses should be studied in some detail by the potential Stage 3 candidate:

- Equine influenza

- Strangles

- Colic

- Tetanus

- Azoturia/equine rhabdomyolysis

- Lymphangitis

In addition there should be knowledge of the following:

- All types of wounds and bleeding

- Parasites (external and internal, including types of worm), their effect and control

- Cracked heels

- Mud fever

- Ringworm

- Lice

- Urticaria

- Warts/sarcoids

Conditions which might affect soundness and action or blemish the horse

- Curbs

- Spavin (bog and bone)

- Splints

- Capped hock/elbow

- Windgalls

- Thoroughpin

- Stringhalt

- Sprains and strains of muscles, tendons or ligaments

- Filled legs

Wind problems

- Whistling/roaring

- Broken wind/emphysema

- Restrictive airway obstruction

- Hobdaying/tubing

- Choking

Nursing a sick horse

Straightforward care of the sick or lame horse would be within the basic remit of a trained groom (competent Stage 3 holder). You will be required to know about:

- Sick nursing procedure to incorporate the full care of the ill or lame horse including the management of his diet.

- Adjusting feed requirements according to reduced work and possible enforced box rest.

- Monitoring the condition of the sick horse, liaising with the vet and carrying out instructions and medication on the vet's advice.

- Recording progress and development under treatment and reintroduction of work as appropriate with a period of rehabilitation relative to the period of lay-off.

Obviously the Stage 3 candidate will not have genuine experience of many of the conditions listed above. The more the candidate has handled horses in work, both stabled and at grass, the more familiar he will be with recognising the healthy horse and therefore aware of anything untoward which might indicate the onset of an illness or lameness.

1.3.6 Organisation of feed store and tack room

Good organisation of the feed room/store and tack room(s) are essential to the smooth and efficient running of a stable yard, small or large. Some considerations should therefore be given to this aspect of stable management.

Looking at the **feed store** first, at Stage 3 competence you should be able to discuss:

- Possible position in the yard relevant to ease of use and convenience.

- Approximate size, depending on the number of horses to service.

- Possible type of flooring (for cleanliness and safety).

- Doors and windows, siting for maximum accessibility and light.

- Types of feed bin.

- Additional features such as feedchart, scales, shelf for additives, cupboards, power point, kettle, boiler, racks for buckets or bowls, etc.

- Possible additional storage facilities for extra food.

With regard to the **tack room**, one of the main considerations must be security, both during the working day and after hours. Points for discussion would include:

- Size, relative to how much equipment is to be stored.

- Possible consideration to provide two tack rooms to accommodate school tack and livery horse tack separately in a commercial yard.

- Provision of security. Overall building including the roof, doors and windows having reliable anti-theft devices installed.

- Provision of a warm and dry enough environment so that tack does not deteriorate during storage.

- Consideration of a hard-wearing but easily maintained floor surface.

- Provision of a power point, good light source and a sink with hot and cold water.

- Provision of separate areas for storage of equipment and an area for cleaning tack.

- Consideration of how saddles and bridles are hung.

- Naming of tack and identifying for security.

- Storage of additional equipment, such as rugs, boots, bandages, spare bits, breaking and lungeing equipment, etc.

- Consideration of how rugs might be stored out of season.

- Consideration of how rugs might be dried, aired or cleaned, and if the latter is not done on site, what provision might be made for it.

Candidates should feel confident about discussing tack rooms and feed stores that they have experience of or have seen in a working yard, recognising their strengths and weaknesses.

1.3.7 Stable design

An understanding of simple stable design is expected at Stage 3 level. This knowledge is sought in the practical oral section and usually involves the examiner walking around the stable yard with the group of candidates, discussing the yard in front of them. It may also be discussed in the stable itself, and here again as a competent Stage 3 person you will be expected to discuss the pros and cons of what is in front of you.

The following aspects of stable design should be considered by the Stage 3 candidate:

- What constitutes a good size for a horse?

- Suitability of building materials, with thoughts on those preferable and why.

- Height of internal ceiling.

- Height and width of doorways.

- Fittings within the stable, to include ideas on rings, water appliances, mangers, racks and lighting.

- Type of floors and drainage.

- Windows – number and size.

- Ventilation appropriate to the type of stable (e.g. American barn type stabling will have different requirements from a simple outdoor stable).

All the above discussion points should reflect personal opinion and practical experience; knowledge of costing of materials is not required.

With consideration for the whole stable yard the following factors might be included in discussion:

- Shape of yard, internal or external stables (open or barn type).

- Yard surface.

bars, appropriate to inside boxes in 'American barn' type stabling, allow horses visibility and air circulation

tie rings (at chest height)

solid walls between horses

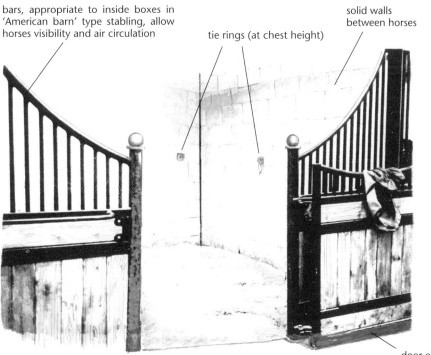

wide doorway for easy, safe access

door opens wide

A 12ft x 14ft internal stable – a good size. This stable has rubber flooring overlaid with a small amount of bedding for comfort and cleanliness.

- Enclosure of yard.

- Siting of muck heap, feed room, tack room, forage and bedding store.

- Additional features such as fire warning signs and fire fighting equipment, mounting block, security lighting or alarm system.

It must be stressed that in this type of discussion it is opinions based on practical experience and good observation which are required of the candidate, rather than definite right or wrong answers. Different candidates will almost certainly offer varying information. Try to volunteer information which reflects your personal experience of a yard in which you have worked, or of which you have some knowledge. Try to be forthcoming and offer as much relevant information as you can on each subject.

1.3.8 Grassland management

As a Stage 3 candidate you should have a clear understanding of the basic care and management of grassland as it relates to the grazing and care of horses or ponies living at grass, or those being turned out to grass for exercise. Simply, the best way to understand the management of grassland for horses is to consider the pasture over a twelve-month period. You should be able to discuss the following topics:

- Harrowing pasture, when and why.

- Rolling, when and why.

- Fertilising, when and why. Basic understanding of the types of fertiliser that might be used on horse pasture.

- Topping, to maintain good growth of the sward.

- Weed and poisonous plant control.

- Basic management of poached or bare areas.

- Fencing, and the reasons for and against the different types.

- The need for access to water and possible options for providing water.

- Use of other animals for cross-grazing and the benefits and disadvantages of this practice.

- The approximate acreage required for keeping one or more horses at grass.

- The reasons for rotating pasture and how this is done.

- Parasite control and how to achieve it.

- How and where to feed horses/ponies living out at grass in winter.

- Extra considerations when caring for 'out' horses/ponies in winter and summer.

Knowledge of amounts of fertiliser and costs per acre are not expected at this level.

You should feel comfortable about discussing management of pasture at any time of the year. In-depth knowledge of pasture management is not expected, but a practical understanding of how grassland must be maintained for maximum benefit to horses is necessary. It is especially helpful if the candidates can relate to their own experience of paddocks or fields that they have helped to maintain. Discussing a real situation of managing a number of horses or ponies which live out at grass adds a confident approach to theoretical information, which must obviously be studied to underpin practical experience.

1.3.9 Psychology of the horse

A true understanding of the horse's nature is what the examiners will be wanting you to show here. Understanding the horse comes from a deep caring about the equine and a desire to know how he thinks and what 'makes him tick'. This caring approach should be intrinsic in anyone wishing to make their career with horses. Greater awareness and deeper understanding of the horse comes with time and constantly 'being around horses'. Understanding of the horse's behaviour should include:

- Knowledge of his behaviour at grass, both alone and in groups of other horses.

- Knowledge of the possible problems with mixing mares and geldings.

- Knowledge of the pros and cons of grouping young and old horses together.

- Possible characteristics which could be identified as problematic for horses living at grass.

In the stable there should be understanding of the characteristics which could be identified as 'vices' or repetitive behaviour syndromes. Certain behavioural symptoms, categorised as the following, should be recognised:

- Weaving.

- Crib biting.

- Windsucking.

- Box walking.

Natural traits associated with the horse's behaviour as a herd animal must be recognised and understood in the context of how we ride, train or generally attempt to achieve harmony with the horse.

The following subjects should be considered when understanding the horse's behaviour when ridden.

- Anxiety apparent in jogging and what this might be a sign of.

- Refusing to jump.

- 'Napping' or refusing to go forward.

- A horse whose behaviour suddenly changes and what this might indicate.

- What might indicate stress, anxiety or nervousness.

- What effect a nervous rider might have on a horse.

- Bad management in terms of either underfeeding or overfeeding and how this might reflect in the ridden horse.

- A horse who rushes his fences.

The Stage 3 candidate should feel confident about discussing aspects of the horse's behaviour in any condition in which the horse might be kept or when being ridden.

1.3.10 General knowledge

General knowledge in the theory section of the Stage 3 examination may cover any of the following subjects;

- Understanding the risks and responsibilities involved with riding on the public highway.

- Safety precautions and fire prevention procedure in the stable yard.

- Correct procedure in the event of an accident or incident in the yard or when riding.

- Knowledge of the aims and objectives of the British Horse Society and the benefits of membership.

- Awareness of the various departments of the British Horse Society (Examinations, Training, Welfare, Safety, Access, Approved Riding Schools and British Riding Clubs) and the role of each.

It is hoped that Stage 3 candidates will already have had a thorough grounding in the horse industry. They must possess an all-round knowledge which would equip them to competently look after several horses, either stabled or at grass. They must show common sense and an aptitude to seek information from a more experienced or knowledgeable person if in doubt as to what to do in any circumstance.

Within the theory section of the Stage 3 exam, all the subjects covered in the previous sections should be examined. The amount of coverage given to each subject may vary from one exam to another and from one examiner to another. It is important to offer as much clear information as possible. Try to avoid feeling intimidated if questions are repeatedly asked on a subject that you feel you have already answered. Continue to try to answer with confidence. Listen carefully to answers given by other candidates in your group and be prepared tactfully to contradict information they have given if you feel sure it is incorrect. If you agree in general with facts that have been given, then say so. Do not repeat information that has already been offered – this just wastes time and detracts from you being able to show your greater knowledge by leaving time for other subjects.

If you make a mistake in what you say and then realise your error, be brave enough to say so. Do not hope that the examiner will not have noticed. The examiners are trained people with years of experience, and although they may not show that they have noticed anything, they almost certainly have.

Try to avoid being influenced by anyone else in your group. It is easy to be pulled down by a weaker candidate, so that you say less (because they are saying less); similarly if there is one vociferous candidate, you must make sure that you get a word in as often you can. In this latter situation, the examiner should control the session so that everyone has an equal opportunity to speak.

If you know that speaking in the theory section is an area that you find difficult, then get as much practice as you can. Practise answering imaginary questions and ask a friend or colleague to test you on various subjects. If possible, get together with other people who can discuss the subjects with you, so that you have practice in a group session.

The theory discussion section will last between 45 minutes and an hour, depending on the number of candidates on the day.

1.4 Horse Knowledge and Care – Practical

THIS IS A TOTALLY practical section. In this part of the Stage 3 examination you should be able to demonstrate ease and confidence in a variety of everyday situations, dealing with horses who are fit and in regular work. The good handling of the horse throughout and awareness of its traits of behaviour are essential. An awareness of safety should also be evident in your manner. Actions such as positioning of the horse safely when picking up hind feet, for example, should be automatic. Attention to detail in any of the following aspects of good management should be visible and ongoing:

- Tying the horse up with a quick-release knot at all times.

- Closing the stable door behind you when in the stable with the horse.

- Skipping out the stable when first going in to deal with a horse.

- Picking out the horse's feet before bringing him onto the yard.

- Picking up droppings into a skip as they appear when working in the stable.

- Giving the horse a pat and a reassuring word at any time when you may be going to do something for which he might need a warning (e.g. picking up a hind leg).

- Making sure that whatever you are doing with the horse you have considered your position in relation to the horse's in the stable, to maximise your safety.

The horses used for the practical section will probably be school or livery horses who may be clipped out (depending on the time of year), fairly fit and in work. It is essential that you are able to show competent handling of the horse throughout. You should handle all equipment safely and with due regard for its cost and the need for maintenance. Horses who become fractious or ill-tempered in the presence of a less competent candidate should be reassured by a good candidate.

The tasks required are designed to allow you to demonstrate your competence as a groom. While there is never a specific time limit placed on the completion of a task, competence is assessed partly with a time factor involved. A person who, for example, can perfectly and immaculately equip a horse with tack for competition, but who takes 45 minutes to complete the task, could not be considered competent at this level. At Stage 3 you must have an industrial speed and efficiency which is commensurate with the level of employability expected by the qualification.

The following text will highlight the requirements of the Stage 3 practical section. The potential candidate must first be trained in correct techniques and then gain sufficient practice under supervision so that the technique becomes fully practised and efficient. This efficiency must then hold good under the scrutiny of examination. There will be some variations in technique depending on who is the trainer. 'Many roads lead to Rome' is a well-worn phrase and one that is acceptable in the horse industry. The criteria for an acceptable technique by which a task may be carried out should be:

- Is it in the interests of the horse's welfare? (i.e. it does not inconvenience the horse in any way)

- Is it safe for both horse and groom/rider?

- Is it clearly identifiable as a means by which someone with less experience or knowledge could safely copy the method and learn?

- Is there clear reasoning behind why it should be done that specific way?

If the answer is yes to all the criteria for a specific technique then it is acceptable. It does not make this method any more correct than another which can also claim the same answer to the criteria listed.

There is no such thing as 'a BHS way'; the BHS way is any way which demonstrates:

- Safe practice.

- Efficient work which is in the best interests of the horse's welfare.

- A recognisable and teachable system to those less knowledgeable.

1.4.1 Fitting tack for work and competition

At Stage 3 level you should be able to choose and fit suitable equipment for:

- A dressage competition (including the fitting of a double bridle).

- A cross-country schooling session.

The choice of an appropriate dressage saddle should include showing some knowledge and opinions about different types of numnah or saddle cloth, and different types of girth and their materials.

You will also need an understanding of the function of a double bridle and some knowledge of different types of appropriate bits with options for types of rein (e.g. plain, laced, half rubber).

When choosing the saddle for riding across country, you will be expected to show some knowledge of the difference in design of a general-purpose saddle and a more forward-cut jumping saddle, including some recognition of modern designs of saddle (e.g. close contact type). Some practical experience of different types of girth and their materials is also required.

You should be able to choose appropriate numnahs for cross-country riding as well as additional equipment such as breastplates/girths, over-girths or surcingles, and martingales.

Candidates should be able to discuss the difference in equipping a horse for a work session as opposed to a competition (i.e. duration, intensity, additional safety requirements, proximity to home).

It should be clear to the examiners that the following criteria are a priority when fitting tack:

- Comfort of the horse.

- Safety of horse and rider.

- Correct fit.

- Awareness of condition and maintenance of all equipment used.

Throughout this section the way in which the horses are managed and handled is of utmost importance. Competent people automatically show an awareness of the horse's attitude and behaviour throughout their work. Correct handling of the horse and a calm, sympathetic manner at all times convey an air of confidence and familiarity with the situation. The competent groom is always efficiently in control of the horse, handling an awkward or fractious horse with firmness and confidence. The placing and management of the equipment also demonstrates competence (e.g. an expensive saddle left casually on a stable door, where it could be pushed off by the horse, does not instil confidence in the observer).

1.4.2 Fitting boots and bandages for work and competition

At this level you should have a familiarity and knowledge of the everyday equipment that is available for protection of the horse's legs. This familiarity is achieved primarily by using such equipment, but also by looking at tack used by riders at competitions, or at boots and bandages on sale in saddlery shops, and by taking every opportunity to observe equipment in current use. Should a piece of equipment be presented to you in the exam, the like of which you have never seen before, then try to work out where the protection might be offered.

When using boots for exercise the following general guidelines apply:

- Straps, whether Velcro or buckle, usually face backwards on the leg. (This principle does not, however, apply to travel boots or knee boots, where often for correct fit the straps must face forwards.) With double Velcro, the first strap will face forwards with the second over-strap facing backwards.

- Usually a broader area of boot will fit the lower part of the leg around the fetlock joint.

- Thickening in the boot may fit on the inside of the leg or may be designed to sit along the tendons at the back of the leg; in the latter case the straps may fit over the front of the leg and the boot may be open-fronted.

The material from which the boots are made is important. There should also be some understanding of how the boots may be maintained after work.

- Is the material washable?

- Does the material cause sweating?

- Is the material tear-proof or resistant to over-reaches?

- Are the straps secure, or do they need reinforcement with tape?

- Would the boots be appropriate for a short period of work or could the horse wear them for several hours?

Knowledge of the use of exercise bandages is required. The candidate should feel confident about discussing the pros and cons of using exercise bandages, including ideas on the materials which might be best used underneath the bandages. Competent and effective application of exercise bandages will be expected. The candidate should be able to apply tape to secure bandages, if required.

There will probably be a variety of different types of bandage available for use in the exam and the candidate should choose the one which is most familiar to them, the one they would be most likely to use at home. It is important that the candidate feels confident to fit a variety of bandages, so that if an exact replica of what they use at home is not available, they still feel confident to fit something similar.

Practice in the use of exercise bandages is essential. If you are not familiar with the regular application of bandages in your day-to-day work, then before the exam it is advisable to fit one at least once a day for a week or more, so that competence is assured. When fitting any equipment during the exam, particularly a bandage, if you feel that it is not satisfactory, remove it swiftly and restart. This is preferable to ending up with something that is less than effective in fulfilling the job required of it.

Within the practical section of the exam, you will be expected to fit an exercise bandage on either a front or hind leg, so make sure that you can do either equally well. You may be asked to choose boots which you would feel are appropriate for cross-country schooling or competition. You will then be expected to fit these. Consider the difference in boots which may be suitable for a short schooling session but which may not be sturdy enough or attach securely enough to withstand a full cross-country course in competition. Similarly consider bandages which might be appropriate for use in dry conditions or indoors, compared to leg protection which might be more suitable for wet or muddy riding conditions.

Don't panic if you see equipment which appears unfamiliar. Instead take a commonsense approach as to where the boot might fit and where the protection would be offered on the leg. A sensible assessment of the material the boot is made from and what type of attachments it has for fitting will assist your opinion of its use. The boot may have a specific name, but it does not matter if you don't know this; if the boot has an obvious maker's name on it then identify this (e.g. Clarendon or Woof). If you really have no idea where the boot might fit then say so; this is preferable to applying the boot in totally the wrong place!

Sensible choice of boots and efficient fitting, along with clear knowledge and understanding of the pros and cons of using a variety of protective wear on horse's legs, is what examiners want to see in this practical section. Neat, workmanlike bandages, applied consistently, are required.

1.4.3 Checking and adjusting equipment for travelling a horse

At Stage 2 level the candidate is required to put on equipment suitable for travelling a horse. At Stage 3, in the practical section, the horse will already be dressed and the requirement will be to check that the tack used is fitted safely and that the candidate would feel comfortable about travelling the horse in it.

The following guidelines could be used to identify the safety and fit of the equipment:

- At first glance does the horse look comfortable and does all the equipment used look appropriate?

- Ideally the horse should be wearing a well-fitted leather headcollar with rope attached.

- The rug chosen should be appropriate to the weather conditions.

- The horse should be wearing four well-applied travelling bandages with suitable padding underneath, or a set of four travelling boots.

- The horse may be wearing a tail bandage, tail guard or other similar tail protection.

- The horse may be wearing a poll guard, especially if travelling in a trailer.

- The horse may possibly be wearing over-reach boots in front, if the travel boots or bandages do not cover the front coronet area of the foot.

- There may possibly be knee and/or hock boots with bandages.

The candidate should be capable of making a quick and efficient assessment of all the equipment, and if necessary advise on any aspect of the fitting that would render the tack unsafe or inadequate on a journey. If appropriate, any piece of equipment that needs adjusting or reapplying should be remedied without question. If the situation arose where a piece of tack was unsafe or inadequate for the journey, the candidate should remove it or advise the examiner.

The horse provided dressed for travel will be the same horse that is used for the loading and unloading task in the practical exam. It is therefore assumed that if the candidate is happy to load the horse, the candidate is also happy with the equipment the horse is wearing.

1.4.4 Checking a vehicle for transporting horses

The ability to check a vehicle for safe travelling, prior to loading a horse or horses, is essential if the care of the horse(s) is to be yours during the journey. Irrespective of who is the driver, it is the groom's responsibility to make sure that the vehicle for transporting horses is well prepared.

The following checks can apply equally to a trailer or lorry, though some of the

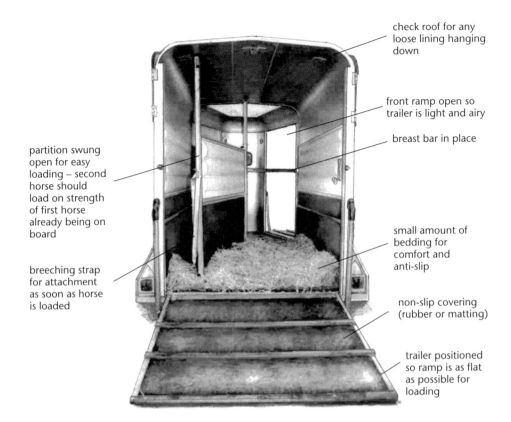

check roof for any loose lining hanging down

front ramp open so trailer is light and airy

breast bar in place

partition swung open for easy loading – second horse should load on strength of first horse already being on board

small amount of bedding for comfort and anti-slip

breeching strap for attachment as soon as horse is loaded

non-slip covering (rubber or matting)

trailer positioned so ramp is as flat as possible for loading

A trailer for travelling one or two horses.

checks would be relevant to the towing vehicle if the transport is a trailer:

- The tax on the vehicle should be current.

- The vehicle must be insured for the person who will be driving.

- There should be regular checks of tyre pressure, oil level, water in the radiator and water in the screen washer bottle.

- If driving at night the lights must all be clean and in good order, including indicators, and fog and hazard warning lights.

- The area in which the horse(s) are to travel should be clean and well ventilated.

- There should be good flooring, with, if necessary, a small amount of bedding down, depending on the type of floor surface.

- There should be safe rings for tying horses, and haynets as required.

- Partitions should move easily and be able to be secured during loading and then safely closed during travel. Breeching straps should be in place in a trailer.

- There should be no loose appendages inside the vehicle, such as damaged roof or wall lining, which could possibly injure the travelling horse(s).

- The ramp should be secure and safe, with suitable ridges or non-slip covering, to prevent slipping when loading.

- There should be safe gates (in a lorry) to enclose the top of the ramp while loading, and to close over the interior of the lorry before the ramp is put up.

- The ramp should be sprung in such a way that it is easy to lift for one person, without possible risk of injury to that person.

When checking the vehicle for safety prior to travelling, you may be asked to do this as a joint exercise with one or more other candidates. In this case it is essential that you give clear information about the part of the vehicle that you have personally checked. Some examiners may allocate each person a specific area to look at, but if this is not the case, you must make sure that you clearly describe the areas that you have looked at. You should say if there are some areas that you have not personally had time to check.

The positioning of the vehicle will also be relevant. If the vehicle is not in an appropriate place for safely loading the horse, this must also be stated.

1.4.5 Loading and unloading horses

The task of loading and unloading horses from a lorry or trailer should be something which is familiar to anyone of Stage 3 competence. It is important that the person feels confident in his ability to load or assist in loading any horse. Generally, horses should be straightforward and easy to load. Inevitably there will be instances when a horse is difficult to load and the reasons for this may be varied, possibly due to a deep-seated fear. Clear ideas on why some horses are awkward to load should also be the remit of the competent Stage 3 groom. Reasons to consider may be:

- Bad previous experience of travelling or rough handling when loading.

- Travelling the horse too fast or without due regard for its balance and comfort on corners and while braking.

- Lack of familiarising the young horse with the experience of travelling and so establishing a pattern of worry rather than confidence.

Loading

It is unwise to load a horse single-handedly unless the horse is well known to load easily without any other assistance. If in doubt, then always load with some help. If loading a horse as a group exercise, then designate the roles for each person before taking the horse from the stable. It is essential that once the task is begun, the horse is loaded with the minimum of fuss and the procedure is carried out smoothly and consistently, with everyone aware of what they should be doing. One candidate must decide what each person's role is to be. You must be aware of your role and be ready to carry it out for a fluent loading exercise.

For an individual loading the following procedure might be appropriate:

- Check that the vehicle is ready, well sited and the partition open.

- Check that the horse is ready and the headcollar is well fitted.

- Lead the horse out of the stable and to the vehicle.

- Lead the horse up the ramp, turn him into position and tie him up.

- Close the partition as necessary. If appropriate, attach the breeching strap.

- If a lorry, close the gates at the top of the ramp. Close the ramp.

- Recheck the horse to make sure he is safely tied and comfortable before leaving.

If two or more people are involved in loading, the procedure would be identical except that there could be one person strategically placed a little behind the horse as he is led up the ramp, in case he shows any reluctance to load. There could be one person (same or additional) to close the partition across, while the person who has led the horse up the ramp stays with the horse until the partition is safely closed. It is important that an excess of helpers does not end up hampering a smooth loading procedure. If necessary additional people could be deployed to unload the horse, so that everyone has been involved with the activity in some way.

Unloading

Unloading a horse(s) is generally less problematic than loading. Similarly, however, if more than one person is to be involved then it is important that everyone knows his role before the unloading starts.

Make sure that the vehicle is safely parked. Avoid unloading horses in an area where there is no safe enclosure, or directly onto a road with busy traffic. There are instances when this is not possible to organise, but greater awareness of the risks involved are essential in these cases.

If unloading alone then the procedure (from a lorry) might be as follows:

- Put down the ramp.

- Undo the ramp gates.

- Undo the partition.

- Untie the horse and lead him down the ramp.

If the horse is liable to become fractious and anxious to leave the lorry in a hurry, it may be preferable to put on a bridle to give extra control when offloading him.

With help, your assistant could undo the ramp, gates and partition while you stay with the horse until it's time to lead him out.

Unloading from a trailer single-handedly is not quite so straightforward unless there is a front ramp, or unless the horse is sensible and very familiar with unloading calmly. If there is a front ramp then the same procedure applies to unloading from a lorry. If backing out of a trailer then probably the safest way to unload is to put the ramp down, then untie the horse, leaving the rope over his neck, while the breeching strap is still in place. Then from behind (standing to the side) undo the breeching strap and coax the horse to come out backwards with you standing near the side of the ramp to guide him out

BELOW AND FACING: BITS COMMONLY SEEN IN EVERYDAY USE

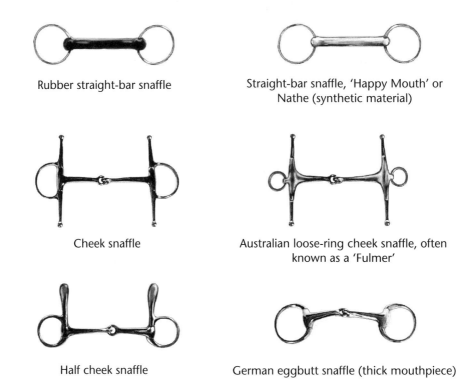

Rubber straight-bar snaffle

Straight-bar snaffle, 'Happy Mouth' or Nathe (synthetic material)

Cheek snaffle

Australian loose-ring cheek snaffle, often known as a 'Fulmer'

Half cheek snaffle

German eggbutt snaffle (thick mouthpiece)

straight, as he leaves the partition. It is then possible to pick up the lead rope to bring him off the last few steps in control. Unloading from a trailer with assistance is easier and definitely preferable.

1.4.6 Bits in everyday use

Throughout the practical section the candidate should feel happy to discuss any piece of tack or equipment which might be considered to be part of the day-to-day running of any commercial or competition yard. This will include bits in common use as well as boots, which have already been discussed.The candidate should be happy to discuss a variety of bits, which fall into several families (e.g. snaffles, double bridles, gags, pelhams, bitless). As with the description of boots, they should feel able to discuss the possible action of different bits, even if they

Eggbutt snaffle (thin mouthpiece)

French link bit

Wire ring (loose ring) German snaffle
(thick mouthpiece)

D snaffle, often known as a 'racing bit'

German KK bit. Central 'lozenge'
in same plane as bit, so very mild.
Similar in action to a French link

Hanging cheek snaffle

THREE SLIGHTLY 'STRONGER' BUT COMMONLY USED BITS

Mullen-mouth pelham
with curb chain

Dr Bristol snaffle. The flat
central plate, being angled,
makes the bit more severe

Three-ring gag snaffle, also
known as 'Dutch gag' or
'bubble bit'

are unable to give the specific name for a particular bit.

When considering the action of a bit, the following criteria may be used:

- Material(s) from which the bit is made.

- Is the bit jointed or unjointed?

- Does the bit have a smooth mouthpiece?

- If not smooth, how is the mouthpiece marked (e.g. twisted, grooved, ridged)?

- Is the mouthpiece thick or thin?

- Is there only one piece of material in the mouth, or more than one?

- What are the rings of the bit like (e.g. eggbutt, loose-ringed, cheeked)?

- How wide is the bit?

- Which pressure points in the mouth or around the head are likely to be affected by this bit?

1.4.7 Care of the competition horse after work

This section could cover dealing with the horse immediately after the competition itself, or after the routine daily work of the competition horse. There are obvious similarities. Away at a competition there are additional factors which might affect the care (e.g. working in unfamiliar surroundings, possible added tension from horse or rider because of competition environment).

The priorities when caring for the competition horse after work are:

- To return the horse to his resting state of comfort (before work started) as reasonably quickly as possible.

- To monitor his well-being and react accordingly to any signs which might indicate that he is not regaining his healthy resting state.

- To provide the horse with the essentials for achieving that state of rest which would be:

  - Walking to regain normal breathing.

  - Cooling.

  - Water to quench thirst and restore body fluids lost through work.

  - Rugs and bandages according to the weather.

  - Food as appropriate.

- Grooming and checking for injury.

■ Considering when to travel the horse home and making provision for his comfort on the journey.

■ Monitoring the horse immediately after work or competition (especially if arduous) and for at least the day after strenuous work.

■ Choosing appropriate gentle exercise for the day after hard work.

■ Monitoring over the next few days to see that the horse has not suffered any after-effects from the work, and adjusting the daily fittening programme if there have been adverse effects.

It is of great benefit to the potential Stage 3 candidate to travel to some competitions as an acting groom. In this capacity you get to experience the handling of horses at competition, and observe how some horses behave differently when away from home in an exciting environment. Attending competitions gives you first-hand experience which is hard to simulate anywhere else. If you are not able to go to competitions with a competitor, then try to attend different types of show as a spectator. Visit the lorry park and observe horses being prepared for competing, then watch the working-in area, which will give much insight into the warming up of horses for different disciplines. Then go to the end of the course (cross-country or show jumping) and watch what is done to the horses on completion of their round.

1.5 Horse Knowledge and Care – Practical Oral

THE PRACTICAL ORAL SECTION of the Stage 3 exam is usually examined by one examiner with a group of between four and six candidates. The section is conducted in a stable with one horse and in parts of the stable yard as appropriate. Each candidate should have an equal opportunity to offer information on each subject. Inevitably one or two candidates may be more forthcoming than others in the group. Whilst the examiner should monitor and control the input from candidates, you must make every effort to volunteer as much factual information as you can. Whilst you run the risk of being asked to stay quiet, this is preferable to having the examiner trying to draw responses from you. Pay attention to the answers of other people and be confident enough to offer your own opinions, especially if you feel that an answer given by someone is incorrect. Make every effort to put across your own thoughts and opinions which you should believe are right, otherwise you may be regarded as agreeing with someone whose answer is in fact incorrect.

1.5.1 The main superficial muscles of the horse

It is sometimes said that learning the complicated names of the superficial muscles of the horse bears no relation to the practical job of caring for horses – so why bother? Someone who can memorise information may not necessarily be very good at caring for the horse in practice. The main aim of encouraging competent grooms to understand the basic physiology of the horse is so that, in the wider context of caring for horses, they will be able to recognise when a horse is not performing at his best, when he might be suffering from a minor pulled muscle, or muscle soreness. This would then enable the competent groom to avoid further problems by dealing with early symptoms, or referring the potential problem to someone in seniority. A small symptom might therefore be prevented from developing into a more significant and serious problem. The same argument can be applied to all the basic knowledge of physiology and anatomy in this practical oral section.

When starting to study the main superficial muscles of the horse, the easiest way to identify with the task is to work systematically over the horse's body learning the muscle names in groups and finding out what part of the body they motivate. The skeleton is the horse's rigid structure, and muscles, tendons and ligaments facilitate the movement of the skeleton.

The superficial muscles should become familiar to you. If you find the names complicated and difficult to pronounce, practise them frequently until they become automatic. Practise identifying them on a horse and from pictures and diagrams. Try naming them in groups and then pick out isolated muscles. Make sure that you can identify them in any order, starting from the head of the horse or from his hindquarters. If you learn the names by rote, you will be in trouble if you have to recall them out of sequence. Learning any facts as a list is fairly fruitless; the whole object of the exercise is to have a greater understanding of how the horse actually moves, and functions. Make sure that you understand the basic function of each muscle.

The following muscles and their function should be familiar for the competent Stage 3 candidate:

Head and neck

- Masseter

- Rhomboideus

- Splenius

- Trapezius

- Sternocephalicus

- Brachiocephalicus

Shoulder/forearm

- Deltoid

- Triceps

- Superficial pectoral

- Radial carpal extensor

- Common digital extensor

- Lateral carpal flexor

Back/barrel

- Latissimus dorsi

- Intercostal

- Longissimus dorsi

- Deep pectoral

Hindquarter

- Gluteal fascia or superficial

- Semitendinosus

- Biceps femoris

- Deep digital flexor

- Digital extensor

SUPERFICIAL MUSCLES – FRONT VIEW

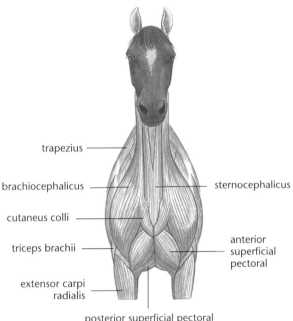

Understanding of the way muscles basically function is important, the principle that muscles work essentially in pairs and that muscles have points of origin, or insertion, onto a bone, sometimes through the attachment of a tendon, should also be understood. The basic difference in physiological structure of muscles, tendons and ligaments should be known. An example of each type of structure and where it could be found in the horse's body would enhance knowledge of the subject. The confident and competent Stage 3 candidate should be able to

SUPERFICIAL MUSCLES

gluteal fascia

lumbo dorsal fascia

biceps femoris

ligamentum nuchae

splenius

rhomboideus

trapezius
(cervical part)

latissimus dorsi

superficial gluteal

trapezius
(thoracic part)

semitendinosus

intercostal

abdominals

masseter

sternocephalicus

serratus

brachiocephalicus

deltoid

anterior superficial pectoral

triceps brachii

biceps femoris

extensor carpi radialis

posterior pectoral

long digital
extensor

deep
digital
flexor

flexor muscle
groups

common digital extensor

lateral digital extensor

describe the siting of the superficial muscles of the horse with a greater understanding of how they enable the horse to move, and what is the difference in
action within the body of muscles, tendons and ligaments.

The discussion on the superficial muscles will take place in a stable with a
horse on which to define the site of each muscle. It is important that the desig-
nation of the muscles is specific. A vague gesticulation in the approximate area
of the body will not be sufficient, nor will a half guess at the name with an apol-

ogy that you find it difficult to remember the exact terminology. The opportunity must be taken if possible for you to demonstrate clearly that you have learnt and understood this aspect of the syllabus, which in the long term is vital to your greater ability to manage the horse in every condition of fitness or work.

1.5.2 Structure of the lower leg below the knee

This is another area of study which should not be neglected. The importance of this knowledge will be far reaching in the long-term competence of the groom, who may ultimately be responsible for horses of all ages in all types of work. Maintaining soundness of horses in work is one of the most fundamental skills of a good horse manager. Lack of knowledge of how the horse is actually put together and functions, will ultimately limit the competence of the carer of the horse.

In conjunction with studying the living limb of a horse, and if possible a cross-section of a preserved leg, the candidate should learn the basic structure of the horse's lower limb from the knee down. It is sometimes interesting to compare the anatomy of the human limb with that of the horse to see how the horse's limb has developed into a 'one-toed' creature from the original five digits present in our own limbs. This comparison may also help the student to understand the bone structure of the horse's limb.

In studying the lower limb it is probably advisable to consider the bones first:

- Cannon bone.

- Two splint bones.

- Two sesamoid bones.

- How the shape of the fetlock joint is formed.

- The long pastern bone.

- The short pastern bone.

- The coffin or pedal bone.

- The navicular bone.

In the hind limb the bone structure below the hock is identical to that of the front limb.

When considering tendons and ligaments in the front limb, knowledge of the following tendons and their points of origin and insertion should be secure:

- The two flexor tendons running down the back of the leg – the superficial flexor tendon, and the deep digital flexor tendon.

- The two extensor tendons running down the front of the leg.

STRUCTURE OF THE
HORSE'S LEG BELOW
THE KNEE

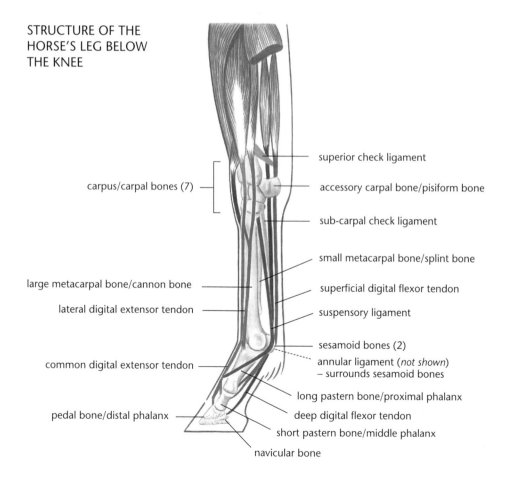

carpus/carpal bones (7)

large metacarpal bone/cannon bone

lateral digital extensor tendon

common digital extensor tendon

pedal bone/distal phalanx

superior check ligament

accessory carpal bone/pisiform bone

sub-carpal check ligament

small metacarpal bone/splint bone

superficial digital flexor tendon

suspensory ligament

sesamoid bones (2)

annular ligament (*not shown*)
– surrounds sesamoid bones

long pastern bone/proximal phalanx

deep digital flexor tendon

short pastern bone/middle phalanx

navicular bone

You are required to know about the following ligaments:

▪ Suspensory ligament.

▪ Check ligament.

▪ Annular ligament (surrounding the sesamoid bones).

In each case the points of origin and insertion of these ligaments should be known, with understanding of how the limb is motivated by the tendons and ligaments in conjunction with the muscles in the upper limb.

The basic structure and understanding of the function of the horse's foot is probably one of the most important areas of the horse's anatomy. It is a well-known fact that when considering unsound horses, the first consideration is always the feet. It is therefore vital that from a very early stage a competent horse carer fully understands this area.

The coronary band is the band of tissue around the top of the foot from which the horn-producing cells originate.

The outer structure of the foot is the insensitive part of the hoof and includes:

▪ The outer wall.

▪ The periople.

▪ The outer sole.

▪ The outer frog.

▪ The insensitive laminae.

The white line visible from the outside surface forms the dividing line between the insensitive parts of the foot and the inner, sensitive parts of the foot.

The inner sensitive parts of the foot include:

▪ Sensitive laminae.

▪ The lateral cartilages.

SECTION THROUGH CENTRE OF FOOT

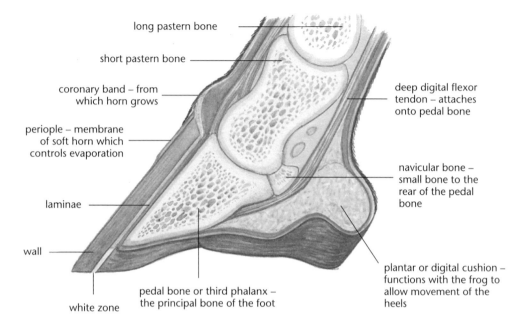

long pastern bone

short pastern bone

coronary band – from which horn grows

periople – membrane of soft horn which controls evaporation

laminae

wall

white zone

pedal bone or third phalanx – the principal bone of the foot

deep digital flexor tendon – attaches onto pedal bone

navicular bone – small bone to the rear of the pedal bone

plantar or digital cushion – functions with the frog to allow movement of the heels

THE SOLE

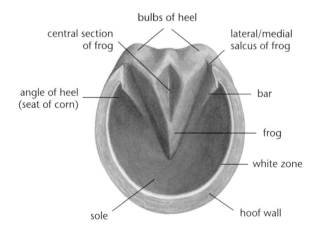

bulbs of heel

central section of frog

lateral/medial salcus of frog

angle of heel (seat of corn)

bar

frog

white zone

sole

hoof wall

- The plantar or digital cushion.

- Ligaments.

- Blood and nerve supply.

At Stage 3 level you should be sufficiently confident to pick up the foot and describe the parts of the foot visible on the underside of the foot and from the outside. You should then be able to designate the internal structures, showing a clear understanding of the inner structure of the foot.

You should have a basic understanding of what happens when the horse puts his foot on the ground. By understanding the locomotion of the horse and the actual function of his feet you will be able to speak with confidence. If a list of names has been memorised with little reference to the living animal, the confidence will be lacking.

As a potential Stage 3 candidate you should gain depth of knowledge about the horse's feet by:

- Watching a farrier working whenever possible.

- Asking questions of both the farrier and vet whenever they are treating feet.

- Being observant to the state of the horses' feet for which you are responsible.

1.5.3 The foot and shoeing

The importance of understanding the structure and function of the horse's foot has been covered in section 1.5.2, and the information following will link comfortably into that detail. The old saying 'No foot, no horse' is a well-used phrase which underlines the need to be able to understand and therefore care for the horse's feet to the best of one's ability. Understanding the structure and function of the feet is the first essential step in good management.

In the discussion on the foot and shoeing in the practical oral section of the Stage 3 examination, you should understand:

- The principle of hoof/pastern axis and the possible effects of this axis being 'broken forward' or 'broken back'.

- The need for the foot to be balanced.

- The possible problems which might arise if the foot is not in balance and the toe is too long.

- What is meant by the terms 'forging' and 'over-reaching', and what can be done about them.

- Whether there is a preference for hot shoeing or cold shoeing.

- What variations in the condition of the horn of the feet may indicate.

You may be asked to identify some types of shoe which are commonly used for remedial purposes:

- Egg bar shoe.

- Bar shoe.

- Rolled toe shoe.

- Wide-webbed shoe.

- Seated-out shoe.

- Threequarter shoe.

- Racing plate.

- Heart-bar shoe.

- Feather-edged shoe.

(Note that some more obscure, old-fashioned remedial shoes (e.g. a patten or rest shoe), though rarely used today, may still exist in some yards.)

As with the identification of bits and boots, the commonsense approach to the shoe is much more important than whether the correct name can be given to the item. When looking at a shoe consider:

- Where the pressure may be exerted when the shoe is in place (wall or sole, evenly or in parts).

- Where the nail holes are situated.

- Whether there are toe clips or quarter clips, or no clips at all.

- The shape of the shoe, which might indicate whether it is a front or hind shoe.

- Any other features which could be described (i.e. material such as plastic, or a possible insert of different metal such as tungsten for added density).

The ability of the resourceful candidate to use common sense and good descriptive powers is always preferred over someone who may know the name of an item but has no ability to back up the memory test with sound, practical information about it. Do not worry about not knowing or recognising more obscure, 'one-off' pieces of equipment.

As a competent Stage 3 candidate you should be able to describe the state of the horse's foot in the practical oral section. You should be able to discuss the state of the shoeing, how recently the horse might have been shod or what indications there are that re-shoeing may be imminent. Any variations on standard shoeing should be noted, e.g. if the shoes have stud holes or permanent road studs in place. You should have an understanding of the use of screw-in studs, the pros and cons of their use and how to maintain shoes for their use. Knowledge of the problems associated with poor or faulty shoeing should be apparent.

1.5.4 Conformation

Assessing a horse's conformation can ultimately only be learned through practice. Practise looking at horses at every opportunity; learn to develop 'an eye' for good and bad aspects of conformation.

Conformation is the horse's bone structure, the way in which his skeleton is uniquely put together to give him the lines and angles of his body on which his musculature, skin and hair are overlaid, to give him the physique which we see as 'the horse'. Being able to assess conformation is being able to see beneath the muscle structure and have an 'x-ray' view of the way the bones are linked together. You may notice, for example, which bones are longer or shorter in relation to each other, or where angles are steeper or more sloping, giving the horse his individual appearance.

While it may be easy to assess small areas of conformation, the horse must always be assessed with the whole structure of the animal ultimately in mind. When assessing the horse's conformation therefore always start with an overall picture of the horse before going into specific areas of detail. Each person will develop his own method by which he can assess the horse. In the long term it is important that what you see can be described to someone else so that they can assess your competence and/or learn from the description that you give. When assessing conformation go about it in a systematic way.

- Give an overview. At this stage briefly describe whether the horse is generally quite well proportioned or whether, for example, he has an over-large head for the rest of his body, or is 'light of bone'.

- Learn terms such as 'light of bone', 'back or over at the knee', 'parrot mouthed', 'short of a rib'. Understand why they are used and employ them in the correct context when you assess a horse.

- Work systematically over the horse's body, probably easiest from his head backwards.

- Describe what is there. Move around the horse easily; avoid standing detached from the horse.

- Be prepared to touch the areas that you are discussing – e.g. define the slope of the shoulder with your hand.

- Either move from the shoulder down the front legs and then continue along the body, or alternatively finish the body in entirety and then describe the legs.

- Be able to pick up from any part of the body and continue discussing where someone else has left off.

- Consider the observations made by other participants. Be prepared to disagree if you think, for example, that the horse has an upright shoulder and someone has described it as sloping. Try to be able to substantiate your opinion by showing why you think the shoulder is upright.

- Be able to describe the conformation of the hind limbs just as well as you are able to discuss that of the front legs. Often candidates are better at discussing the front legs, knowing that more often than not the examiner will start at the front of the horse.

- It is essential for your own confidence and competence that you are able to describe any part of the horse's conformation when asked.

- Try to start or finish your section of the discussion with a general reference to the overview of the horse.

The discussion on conformation will be done with a group of four to six candidates. Ideally it should be done outside, with plenty of space for everyone to move around the horse. This may not always be possible if the weather is bad, and the group may be confined to a stable. In this case be sure that you make the observation that assessing conformation is much easier to do in a bigger space, where it is possible to stand back from the horse and observe him as a whole, as well as move in around him.

There is no substitute for practice. Take every opportunity to discuss a variety of horses' conformation on any occasion, with someone more experienced, who can listen and assist in developing your eye for good and bad aspects of conformation. Be aware that some weaknesses in conformation are regarded as more unacceptable than others. The candidate must be able to discuss aspects of conformation which might affect the soundness or the ride of the horse. Ultimately it is how the horse performs, his attitude to his work and his ability to maintain soundness, often in spite of apparent weaknesses in his basic conformation, which dictate the success of that individual throughout his life.

1.5.5 Assessing action and soundness

This task will be carried out as a group exercise with between four and six candidates. As described previously, it is important that each candidate is confident enough to volunteer information as and when appropriate. Either the examiner will allocate one candidate to lead the horse out and then trot it up for observation, or it may be left to the group to designate one member to lead the horse. If one candidate is the handler, he will be given the opportunity to contribute to the discussion at a later stage.

If you are the designated handler of the horse create a workmanlike impression by leading the horse competently in hand and running him up actively. It is almost impossible to observe soundness and action in a horse that is barely putting one foot in front of the other through idleness.

Practice is an essential part in developing skill in assessing the way horses move and to be able to decide on their action and soundness. The more horses that can be observed walking and trotting in hand, on a flat surface, in a brisk active pace, the better the 'eye' will become in assessing the way of going.

In assessing a horse for action and soundness, a systematic approach will help to eliminate the risk of 'missing the obvious'. A methodical way of tackling the task will always gain credit, even if the final observation of soundness is not quite accurate.

- If possible, observe the horse in the stable over the door, for basic stance and attitude.

- If possible, make a brief assessment of the horse in the stable to include running hands (ungloved!) down all four legs to feel for heat, swelling or a painful reaction to pressure.

- Pick up the feet and pick them out before the horse leaves the stable. Note the shoes.

- As the horse is led out of the stable watch for any initial stiffness or reluctance to move.

- Stand the horse up outside the stable again to watch the way he distributes his weight.

- If leading the horse yourself then listen to the footfalls, which can help to give you an indication of unlevelness.

- If the horse is led up for you, ask the leader to walk away from you, turn the horse (away from them) and walk back towards you.

- Observe the walk away from you; particularly watch how the horse turns, whether he saves himself in the turn, and watch him towards you and past you.

- Repeat the same in trot, asking the handler to leave the head free and unrestricted by a tight rein.

- The first consideration must be the regularity and freedom of the gaits.

- The walk should be regular and purposeful, the steps should be picked up and put down actively.

- In trot, the steps should be regular and lively with a feeling of a moment of suspension when all four feet are off the ground.

- If there is any irregularity in the gait, it will probably be most visible in trot.

- If the head nods as the horse approaches you, the horse is probably favouring the leg opposite to the side the head is nodding (i.e. he is taking more weight on the good leg and he drops his head on this side as he saves the weight on the lame leg).

- If the hip drops as the horse moves away from you then similarly he is taking more weight onto the side where the hip is dropping, to save the other leg because it hurts.

- Assuming that the gaits are regular, then the way the horse's limbs actually move can be considered.

- Try to observe the actual flight path of the limb, from the moment it picks up, as it passes through the air and as it returns to the ground.

- Is that flight path straight or does it deviate? If it deviates then how does it deviate?

- How is the weight then taken over the foot when the foot comes to the ground? This will help tell you about the balance of the horse's weight over the foot itself.

Practice will ensure that you become proficient at observing the different ways in which horses move and are able to describe what you see. As a competent Stage 3 person you must be able to confidently describe the action of the horse you are watching as it happens. You must be able to stand by your opinion and be confident enough to say the horse is sound if you think it is. The horse may show stiff, pottery or rather restricted lazy movement but unless there is definite inconsistency in the rhythm of the gait (especially trot) the horse is not actually lame. Describe what you see – if the horse is lazy, apparently stiff or restricted in its movement, then say so.

1.5.6 Assessing sites of lameness and/or injury

As described in the previous section, a systematic approach to examining the horse for any possible sites of unsoundness or injury is the best way to ensure that if there is anything to find it will not be missed.

A systematic method for assessing action has been discussed. This thorough observation of the horse's limbs and feet can be detailed further.

- Observe the way the horse stands (at rest and static, i.e. not moving).

- Decide whether the horse's weight distribution is even over all four limbs or apparently favouring or saving one limb.

- If there is one obvious limb which is uncomfortable, then start any examination with this leg.

- If the troubled limb isn't obvious, then start at the front and look at both front legs, then both back legs.

COMMON SITES OF INJURY AND BLEMISH   * = soft swelling/bursal enlargement

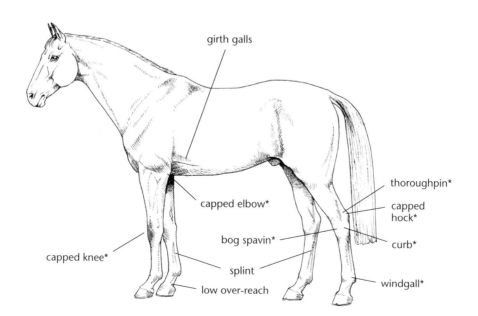

girth galls

thoroughpin*

capped hock*

capped elbow*

bog spavin*

curb*

capped knee*

splint

windgall*

low over-reach

- Always compare both front legs and feet, or both back legs and feet, since any abnormality is easier to gauge against another limb.

- Work from the foot upwards.

- Pick out the feet and notice the state of the shoe and any apparent displacement which might have caused injury.

- Compare the walls of both feet: the temperature of both should match.

- Work up the leg. Feel around the joints for any heat, swelling or pain on pressure, and look for any visible sign of injury.

- If any abnormality is found then compare the two limbs to see how different the abnormal limb is.

The candidate should be observant. Good observation comes from plenty of practice. Handling the horse and examination of the limbs should be carried out with confidence and efficiency. Firm feeling of the limbs is essential. It is also important to realise when a horse is reacting to contact as opposed to showing pain or discomfort from pressure. Some horses are very wary about being examined; they may even overreact because they imagine you are hurting them! It is important that through experience and good handling the competent Stage 3 groom recognises the difference and can assess the 'anxious' horse.

It is absolutely imperative that this examination is done with bare hands. Under no circumstances must gloves be worn for any type of manual assessment of sites of lameness and/or injury.

There should be clear understanding of the difference between soft, fleshy swellings and their causes, and hard, bony developments and their likely causes.

The following conditions should be understood and the site of their occurrence should be familiar to you.

Bony inflammation or enlargements

- Splint.

- Bone spavin.

- Side bone.

- Ring bone.

- Sesamoiditis.

- Pedalostitis.

Soft swellings

- Windgalls.

- Bog spavin.

- Thoroughpin.

- Big knee.

- Capped hock or elbow.

- Curb.

- Tendon injuries.

- Bruises from kicks.

- Muscle pulls or strains.

The Stage 3 candidate should be able to pinpoint on a horse the potential locations of any of the above conditions and actually recognise if the horse has any of these blemishes.

   You should be confident to discuss possible causes of any of the listed conditions. You should know how to manage a horse which might be suffering from any of these problems, and happy to discuss treatment, possible aftercare, and prevention of re-occurrence.

Good observation skills, which stem from practice and a desire not to miss anything, are essential. A competent Stage 3 groom would not miss things like:

- A missing shoe on an otherwise fully shod horse.

- Risen clenches on one or more shoes.

- Feet which look odd and are clearly not a pair (front or back).

- One foot which has white horn while the other three are black. (Merely a point of observation, not necessarily a problem.)

- A horse that is shod in front and not behind. (There may be several reasons for this; try to think what they might be.)

- A horse that has stud holes in his back shoes.

- A horse that has any variation in shoeing from the 'normal', standard-type shoe.

If there is any blemish or abnormality then the candidate should make the following observations:

- Where is the blemish?

- Is it soft or hard?

- Is it hot or cold?

- When pressed does it cause pain or not?

- When felt is it movable (under the skin) or fixed (more deep seated).

- Is it in close proximity to a moving joint with which it is likely to interfere?

- Does it impede any other part of the horse's movement?

Remember that while injuries are most commonly found on the limbs and in the feet, they can occur higher on the horse's body. It is therefore important to check the whole body before confirming an opinion that the horse is uninjured. Always check for cuts and abrasions after the horse comes in from the field, and be aware of injuries which may occur as a result of ill-fitting tack or equipment.

Sites for injuries from poor fitting tack might include:

- Injuries in the region of the withers.

- Injuries in the region around the poll or the top of the head.

- Injuries around the mouth (from an ill-fitting bit).

- Injuries around the girth region.

As previously stated, it is important that you feel confident enough to describe the horse that is in front of you. Be prepared to move up to the horse, feel him carefully and then give your own opinions clearly and with conviction.

1.5.7 Circulatory system

As previously explained, knowledge of the horse's body systems in isolation may seem unnecessary, as if you are learning facts for the sake of them. However, if this knowledge is incorporated into the larger practical application of actually caring for horses in differing types of work and condition, in stables and at grass, it can be invaluable in expanding your competence as a carer. This greater knowledge and competence will enhance your ability to manage the horse to maximum effect with minimum use of the technical expertise of such professionals as the vet or the farrier. It can also greatly improve the management of the horse in all circumstances, enabling minor variations in condition to be noticed at the earliest stage. Thus the time a horse might be off work can be minimised, and minor problems can be prevented from developing into more serious conditions.

The horse's circulatory system is the transport system of his body. The candidate should be familiar with the functions of the system, namely:

- To carry oxygen from the lungs to all parts of the body.

- To remove carbon dioxide from all parts of the body and return it to the lungs.

- To carry water and nutrients from the gut to all parts of the body.

- To remove waste products from the body and transport them to the kidneys.

- To transport hormones from the endocrine glands to other parts of the body.

- To assist in the body's defence as necessary.

- To assist in controlling body heat as necessary.

The candidate should understand the basic constituents of blood:

- Plasma.

- Red blood cells.

- White blood cells.

You should understand that the red cells contain haemoglobin, which has the capacity to combine with either oxygen or carbon dioxide to carry these gases around the body to and from the muscle areas, the site of energy production.

You need a clear understanding of the structure and function of the heart. The four chambers of the heart, their names, the way the blood circulates through the heart and its relationship with the lungs must be known.

The resting heart rate of the average horse is in the region of 35 to 40 beats per minute; this can rise to at least 200 under intense exercise.

You need to understand the basic difference between arteries and veins.

- In all cases except that of the pulmonary artery, arteries carry blood laden with oxygen. Since arteries always leave the heart, they therefore have a stronger pulse due to their close proximity to the pumping action of the heart. The pulmonary artery does leave the heart but is carrying deoxygenated blood back to the lungs.

- Similarly, in all cases except that of the pulmonary vein, veins carry blood laden with carbon dioxide, and veins always return to the heart. The pulse is less strong in veins as they are returning to the heart and therefore are not in close proximity to its pumping action. The pulmonary vein does return to the heart but is carrying oxygenated blood from the lungs to the heart.

- Pulmonary circulation is involved in supplying blood to and from the lungs.

- The whole system is called the systemic system.

The competent Stage 3 candidate should be familiar with all the major veins and arteries (which are always paired) and the major organs they supply.

- Pulmonary (vein and artery) – Lungs.

- Hepatic – Liver.

- Renal – Kidney.

- Mesenteric – Intestine.

- Aorta – Main artery from the heart.

- Vena cava – Main vein to the heart.

The Stage 3 candidate should also understand the importance of the **lymphatic system.** This system runs in tandem with the blood system and is sometimes known as the white blood system. Its main function is to support the blood system in maintaining general cellular good health.

In the practical oral section of the Stage 3 exam the competent candidate should feel confident to indicate on the horse's body approximately where the heart would be found – on the left side of the chest cavity in the area behind the horse's left elbow. You should then feel happy to discuss how blood circulates around the body, starting from the heart. You should be able to listen carefully to input from other candidates and if necessary correct errors of description, before continuing at any point where a previous candidate may have been asked to stop. You must be able to discuss:

- The difference between arteries and veins.

- How blood from an artery and a vein might vary in appearance and production from a wound.

- What the four chambers of the heart are called.

- How the blood flows through the four chambers of the heart.

- What the valves are called between the chambers and how they basically function.

1.5.8 Respiratory system

As discussed in the last section, the student studying for the Stage 3 examination should consider all the horse's systems and the way they interact with each other to provide good health. The respiratory system links very closely with the circulatory system previously discussed. The two systems work in tandem and complete harmony for the efficient functioning of the healthy horse. Understanding how these systems operate will equip the candidate with the ability to recognise any malfunction and deal with it at an early stage, thus preventing further damage to, or lack of performance from, the horse.

The primary function of the respiratory system is to access oxygen from the air, take it into the horse's body and transfer it into the bloodstream, where it can then be transported by the circulatory system.

You need to understand that the respiratory system also:

- Removes carbon dioxide from the blood.

- Helps control body temperature by taking in cool air and breathing out warm air.

- Controls some of the water content of the body – water is constantly being breathed out with deoxygenated air.

The parts of the horse's body directly associated with the respiratory system are:

- Nostrils.

- Nasal cavities.

- Epiglottis.

- Pharynx.

- Windpipe/trachea.

- Larynx.

- Bronchi – the windpipe separates into two bronchi, one bronchus passing to each lung.

- Lungs.

- Bronchioles.

- Alveoli – the many small air sacs where gaseous exchange takes place in the lung tissue. (A single cell is known as an alveolus.)

Each lung is enclosed within an elastic membrane known as the pleura. Inflammation of this lung membrane is associated with the condition known as pleurisy.

Candidates must understand the principle by which air is breathed in through the nasal tract and down the windpipe into the lungs. They should feel confident that they can describe how the air exchange takes place in the alveoli and that the oxygen/carbon dioxide is constantly diffusing through the cell walls into the finely branched capillaries or blood vessels which permeate all the lung tissue. A two-way exchange is constantly occurring throughout the horse's life. The denial of oxygen to the horse for more than just a few minutes, as with any mammal, would cause death very soon after.

There must be awareness of inspiration (breathing in) and expiration (breathing out) and the possible problems that can arise in horses when there is any injury, infection or restriction in the horse's ability to breathe in as much air as he requires for the activity being asked of him.

The following conditions, treatments, etc. related to respiration should be studied and understood:

- High blowing.

- Whistling/roaring.

- Restrictive airway obstruction (RAO).

- Emphysema/broken wind.

- Chronic obstructive pulmonary disorder (COPD).

- Hobday's operation (for whistling or roaring).

- Tubing.

- Allergic reactions to, for example, dust in hay or bedding.

- What problems might arise with respiration if the horse works on a full stomach?

In the Stage 3 exam, you may be asked to describe on the horse in front of you the different locations of the parts of the respiratory system. You may be expected to discuss breathing, and the possible reasons why the respiratory rate of the horse might change.

Assessment of the horse in front of you with regard to its resting respiration rate might be discussed, and you should be capable of deciding what the respiration rate is. At rest the expected rate would be somewhere in the region of 8 to 12 inhalations and expirations per minute.

1.6 Horse Knowledge and Care – Lungeing

1.6.1 Lungeing for exercise

The first consideration in this section is whether the horse has been competently and adequately exercised. The exercise should be such that if it was the only activity that the stabled horse was having on that day, it would be sufficient that the next day the horse would not be sharp and full of himself, as if he had had insufficient exercise the day before.

The lunge horse provided should be obedient and will have been regularly lunged before (you will not be presented with a young, untrained horse). However, it may be a fit and forward-going horse. At Stage 3 level you should be able to lunge a fit horse in work and provide him with adequate exercise on that day.

The choice of paces for exercising a horse on the lunge could include walk, trot and canter on both reins. The candidate would not necessarily be asked to canter the horse. However, a person of Stage 3 competence should be capable of using canter as a gait for exercise. You should not appear concerned if the horse goes into canter voluntarily because he is feeling a bit cheerful or full of himself. You should be able to control and use the energy that the horse may offer.

At Stage 3 you should demonstrate a well-established familiarity with the equipment and show consistent skilfulness when handling the rein and whip, particularly when changing the rein. You need to show a more effective competence overall than someone of Stage 2 level. This competence is only achieved through practice, so it is essential that you gain plenty of experience of actually lungeing a variety of horses for exercise.

You should be prepared to answer questions related to lungeing for exercise:

- How long would you lunge for exercise? (Depends on fitness of horse, but 20–30 minutes for a horse in medium work.)

- Where would you lunge? Type of surface? Enclosed? If not enclosed, then where?

- How do you recognise when the horse has exercised sufficiently?

- Are you able to discuss the basic quality of the gaits? (Forwardness and regularity.)

- Can you show an understanding of the size of the circle and its relevance to the quality of the horse's way of going?

1.6.2 Lungeing equipment

The horse provided for the lungeing section of the Stage 3 exam will be already tacked up. It is each candidate's responsibility to check the fit and suitability of the equipment, change it if appropriate (basic adjustment such as position of a noseband) and comment on it before commencing the lungeing exercise.

The horse should be wearing:

- Saddle or roller. (Stirrups should be secured to prevent slipping down.)

- Bridle. (Reins secured.)

- Lungeing cavesson. (May be leather or nylon).

- Lunge rein. (This may be a web, nylon or rope rein.)

- Side-reins. (Attached to roller or girth but clipped back, not in use. Side-reins may be plain leather or variations of some type with elasticity.)

- Brushing boots. (Full set of four preferably; discuss if only two or none.)

- Over-reach boots. (Optional.)

- Whip of adequate length with a long thong in good condition.

By now you may have preferences for which type of lunge rein or which side-reins you prefer, however you should be able to lunge effectively with any type

Horse 'dressed' for exercise on the lunge (without a rider).

of equipment. You must be able to comment, if for example the cavesson is ill-fitting, or if the side-reins will not adjust appropriately. The slight variations in equipment should not affect you from carrying out an adequate session of exercising the horse on the lunge.

As a competent Stage 3 candidate you will be expected to show consistency in your handling of the lunge rein at all times. Exactly how you hold the rein will have developed from personal preference and ease of handling. Several methods are equally acceptable; no one method is more correct than another. The criteria for any acceptable method of handling equipment (in this case the lunge rein) must be:

- Is the method safe for both horse and handler?

- Is the method effective (enables the job to be done competently)?

- Is the method in the best interests of the horse (i.e. it does not in anyway inconvenience him)?

- Is the method easily transferred as a skill to someone else? Is the method teachable or able to be copied safely by someone without the same knowledge or experience?

- Is the method chosen understood by the person using it, so that he can defend its use and therefore transfer knowledge elsewhere in due course?

The British Horse Society recognises these criteria for competence in its examination system. There is no such thing as 'the BHS way' only in as much as the BHS way embraces the following doctrine:

'Safety, efficiency and understanding of the method, leading to competence through good and consistent practice.'

When lungeing any horse at any time the handler should always wear gloves. When lungeing young, difficult or unknown horses, wearing a hard hat (with chin strap done up) would be a wise precaution. Safe footwear (as when riding) is essential, as would be no flapping clothing (e.g. open coat or a loose scarf). As with any handling of horses, the minimum of jewellery is also sensible. It is unwise to lunge a horse while wearing spurs.

1.6.3 Lungeing site, and safety

Lungeing site

The area chosen for lungeing a horse is very important, however choice of site may be limited by strictures. Ideally the area should be:

- Enclosed, indoors or outdoors.

- If outdoors then the fencing should be quite high and secure.

- Surface underfoot should be level and consistent.

- Grass is perfectly acceptable if level and consistent; grass is preferable to a false or inconsistent artificial surface.

- A gradient has to be managed if used for lungeing. The lunger will have to be aware of the variations in the horse's balance when he is going 'uphill' or 'downhill'.

- If there is no available enclosed area then a corner of a field may be the next best thing, a 'psychological' barrier of raised poles around the area may give a more designated working space and better control.

Safety

Safety is effected by competent lungeing. There are other factors which can relate to the safe lungeing of a horse for exercise and therefore should be considered when taking the horse to work.

- The equipment should be well fitting, comfortable and secure.

- The handler should be safely dressed, as discussed in the last section.

- The area to be used for lungeing should be free from unnecessary obstacles, such as spare jump stands or loose poles.

- The handler should be aware of weather conditions which might have an effect on the horse's behaviour (e.g. strong gusty winds or driving rain); whether indoors or outside these could have an adverse effect.

- The handler should be aware of influences such as other horses in the same schooling area, or horses turned out in an adjoining field.

- Lorries in the car park, traffic on the road nearby – anything unexpected may influence behaviour.

- The fitness of the horse may affect performance.

You will be expected to take a horse to a designated area and lunge him effectively for exercise. You must be able to deal with all eventualities within the remit of exercising a trained lunge horse sufficiently for his only session of work that day.

1.6.4 Deciding on the lunge work

The competent Stage 3 candidate should be capable of choosing the work best suited to effectively exercise the horse.

Having checked the equipment, lungeing can commence on one rein (either left or right to start with is fine). If the horse is biddable and quiet then it is sensible to start in walk. Preferably move the horse onto as big a circle as possible (15–20m) Then proceed into trot and aim to get the horse going forward as soon as possible onto as large a circle as you can and in a consistent rhythm.

Lungeing is effected by competent coordination of voice, rein, whip and body language. It is therefore very important that coordination is effectively established at the earliest opportunity. Confident use of the voice is vital. It is not so much what is said, but how it is said that influences control. You must be positive with your voice and learn to use it in a variable way to gain respect and control.

The following procedure could be an acceptable way to develop the exercise.

- Move the horse out onto the circle, in walk if quiet, in trot if the horse appears lively and full of himself.

- Give the horse a clear voice aid to trot and work the horse in trot forward and rhythmically.

- Make transitions from trot to walk and back again quite frequently to begin to exercise the horse effectively.

- After a few minutes make a change of rein and proceed with the same work on the other rein.

- Aim throughout for obedience in the transitions, forwardness in the gaits and rhythm in all paces.

- Aim for a consistent-shaped circle as large as is possible.

- Be aware of how large a circle you are using when you discuss this with the examiner; often, candidates have little idea of the size of the circle they have been using.

- Aim to be consistent with the handling of the rein and whip throughout your work.

- Make frequent changes of rein so that you work the horse evenly on both reins.

- Once the horse is forward in trot on both reins then attach the side-reins and continue to exercise the horse forward into the reins.

- The horse should work confidently into the side-reins if you have him going forward enough.

1.6.5 Dealing with lungeing problems

When lungeing a horse there are many occasions when the horse does not behave in an easy, controlled way. Often this feels far worse when the horse is on the end of a lunge rein. It is very important that through a positive, confident but calm approach, authority is affirmed and the lunger maintains control and begins to influence the horse's behaviour if he has been sharp and full of himself. When the horse is misbehaving, he will tend to ignore the lunger and may drop his shoulder and cut in on the circle, possibly even bucking and kicking. At this stage, even in an exam situation, do not panic. Some of the following circumstances may well arise at this point:

- The circle becomes inconsistent and variable.

- The horse does not maintain either a steady contact on the rein, or a consistent rhythm on the circle.

- The rein contact may be so variable that the rein becomes briefly slack and may even touch the floor as the horse drops the contact and 'does his own thing'.

- The horse runs in and out of canter and is disobedient to the basic transition commands.

When any of these circumstances arise, the first priority must be to stay in control and avoid actually letting go of the horse. The following points should help to regain control and obedience.

- If normally the rein is held in one hand, put both hands onto the rein, one hand in front of the other to give greater security.

- Transfer your weight back (shoulders back) and take up a braced position, with one heel into the ground, knees bent and a position similar to that you would adopt to sit on a shooting stick. This will help prevent the horse from pulling you forward out of balance.

- Vary your voice aids positively and firmly.

- If the whip is still forward then put it quickly under your arm behind you. (Do not put it down; you may need it in a moment when the horse decides to calm down.)

- With the whip behind you, you can then concentrate on your voice and body stance to assert control.

- Sometimes short, sharp jerks on the rein may prevent the horse from leaning heavily against it. However, it should be remembered that the cavesson sits on a sensitive part of the nose, and it is not in the interests of the horse's welfare to abuse him with the cavesson by giving harsh jerks along the rein.

- Avoid bringing the horse in on an ever-decreasing circle where he may damage himself by interfering or strain himself on too small a circle.

- Avoid running him against a wall. This usually causes greater anxiety as the horse feels trapped by the barrier.

Ultimately persistence and confidence in voice and body language should reaffirm the handler's authority and the lungeing can then proceed.

The way in which the problems are dealt with is always the governing factor when assessing overall competence. Minor lapses of technique when dealing with problems are never the criteria for deciding on an efficient exercise session or otherwise. Faults such as the following are always assessed in the overall context of the performance as a whole:

- Stepping backwards.

- Dropping the whip.

- Letting the rein touch the floor.

- Letting the rein become twisted.

- Letting go of the horse (worst case scenario!).

1.6.6 Assessing the lungeing procedure and talking about it

By the time you have reached this level, you should be capable of assessing the lungeing procedure as it is happening. Ideally you should be able to adapt the choice of work, according to the way the horse is behaving, so that the horse is well exercised. At the end of a lungeing session you should be able to discuss what you have done, how the work progressed and what were the successful results. You should also be able to comment on areas of the work which perhaps did not go as planned and talk confidently about what your approach might be on a future occasion. You must remember that horses on exam days do not have any idea of the importance of the day. Horses will be horses, and they behave according to many influences, so you must be positive enough to describe shortcomings in the performance and not see them as automatic points of failure. Often the way you deal with or discuss a problem will earn you credit for your competence and constitute a pass, even though the practical demonstration of lungeing was not outstanding.

In assessing the performance the candidate should be aware of:

- Whether the horse was forward in his response.

- Whether the horse was sharp, disobedient, not listening and even running away.

- Whether the horse was lazy and therefore behind the lunger's aids.

- Whether the horse worked in a consistent rhythm in his gaits.

- Whether the horse maintained a good circle on both reins, staying into a steady and consistent contact in the rein.

- Whether the horse showed more suppleness or stiffness on one rein than the other.

- Whether the paces varied greatly from one rein to the other.

- How well the horse coped with the work, both mentally and physically.

While a Stage 3 candidate is not expected to age any of the horses or know how old a horse might be, they should recognise basic lack of physical fitness and the horse showing 'green' or youthful behaviour.

Similarly if the horse is obviously older and maybe stiffer as a result, then this observation would be justified. In discussing the horse it is important to suggest that 'perhaps the horse is older and so this could be a reason for the signs of apparent stiffness', rather than 'the horse is stiff because he is old'. The latter observation could only be made if the candidate knew definitely that the horse was old.

The candidate is likely to be asked some of the following questions:

- Was the equipment on the horse satisfactory? If not, what would you want to change?

- Was the area to be used for the lungeing exercise suitable? If not, what would you like to change?

- Were you happy with the way the horse behaved?

- How long do you think the horse should work for to be well exercised?

- Were you happy with the way the horse worked for you? If not, why not?

- What were you looking for in the way the horse went?

- When or why did you decide to put on the side-reins?

- How did you adjust the side-reins? What criteria influenced you?

At Stage 3 level you should demonstrate a consistent and secure technique when handling the equipment for lungeing a horse in regular work for exercise. The horse should be well exercised, the candidate should show understanding of how and when to use the side-reins. You should be able to adjust them correctly and to good effect. In discussion, you must demonstrate knowledge and understanding of the value of lungeing as a means of exercise. Your performance should demonstrate a good practical ability, being able to deal with any minor lapses in behaviour from the horse, which might be regarded as in keeping with a healthy, fit horse feeling well. Similarly if you are lungeing a lazy horse, you must be competent and confident enough to use a positive voice, manner, body language and if necessary appropriate timing and use of the whip to motivate an idle horse. Ultimately it is practical ability and effect that is a priority for competence at Stage 3, linked to an awareness and overall management of safety of both horse and handler in all circumstances.

Part 2

The Preliminary
Teaching Test

Understanding the PTT

Please refer also to the information given under the heading, 'Understanding the Stage 3 Exam' in Part 1

YOU WILL, BY NOW, HAVE SOME EXPERIENCE of taking exams, either in taking your BHS Stage 1 and 2, or through Pony Club tests or NVQ assessment and verification, but the PTT will be the first time that you are examined as a **teacher**.

It is helpful during your training if you can have had some genuine experience of riders who are novices or even complete beginners. This experience may be gained in the following ways:

- Observation in a commercial riding school of weekly riders at different levels and age.

- Some experience of leading novice children or adults in a riding school under the supervision of a qualified person can be very beneficial.

- Helping novice or beginner riders to lead their horses to the school, adjusting stirrups and girths and then helping them at the end of a lesson.

These opportunities allow you to appreciate how limited the complete beginner's knowledge may be. This should help you to remember to teach every aspect of a lesson subject and never assume that a rider knows something already.

As with the Stage 3 exam, carefully study the syllabus and discuss with whoever is training you where your areas of strengths and weaknesses may be. Make a plan for effectively covering the areas which are weaker. For example, if you are nervous about standing up to give your short lecture, take every opportunity to practice this by talking to groups of friends, family or informal gatherings so that you can develop confidence.

Remember that confidence comes from practice and, just as with your riding and stable management, learning to teach takes time.

You must feel confident about:

- Projecting your own voice from the start of the lesson.

- Teach according to what is happening in front of you, not to a stereotyped plan which may not apply to the pupils you have.

- Adhering to clear basic principles such as good basic position, application of the aids and control and understanding of the horse.

- Progressing the lesson in the way you believe is in the best interests of the class or individual, **NOT** because you think the examiners want to see you do something particular.

The examiner will be looking for competence in teaching correct basic principles.

- You must demonstrate self-confidence.

- You should show an ability to project your voice both indoors and outside.

On arrival at the exam centre for your Preliminary Teaching Test, you will be briefed by the chief examiner, who will introduce the team of examiners for the day. The day's events will be explained to you and there will be a programme clearly listed for your benefit. The chief examiner will give each candidate a piece of paper on which there will be:

- A number.

- A subject for your class lesson.

- A subject for your five-minute lecture.

- Whether you are required to give a lead rein or lunge lesson in the afternoon.

Your turnout should be as for the Stage 3 riding section. It is not essential for you to teach wearing your riding hat; it is acceptable for you to leave it by the side of the school (and also a whip) if you prefer. If you are happier keeping both with you (and/or your hat on) then that is your choice.

If it is very cold or you are teaching outside, then a top coat (waterproof if necessary) is sensible. The top coat should be clean, in good repair and not 'loud' in colour or flapping, which might startle the horses.

I emphasise again that the examiners will be looking for a basically sound teaching ability. You must be able to:

- Control your pupils.

- Progress your pupils to some benefit and improvement.

- Maintain an audible voice throughout.

- Deal with simple situations as they arise (e.g. if a horse is apparently lame, you must comment on it; if a rider appears worried, you must attempt to address the problem).

- You must demonstrate a competence to discuss basic lesson plans for a variety of teaching situations.

If at any stage the examiner feels that you are drifting away from developing your lesson satisfactorily, then he or she may suggest that you take a certain path (e.g. introduce jumping position if you are giving a jump lesson and have spent rather too long on the flat). Always regard this as a help, not an interference – the examiner is aiming to help you to show your best and is usually more aware of the time limitations of the exam than you are.

Once you have achieved your PTT it is hoped that you will develop your teaching skills under some supervision as you accrue your 500 hours of practical teaching experience.

2.1 The Class Lesson

2.1.1 Introduction

You will be required to teach a group of riders (usually three or four) for between 35 and 40 minutes. The riders should be capable of walk, trot, canter and riding over small fences, and could be assessed as being about BHS Stage 2 level of ability. The lesson will take place in an area of at least 20m x 40m. Usually the riders will be already mounted and either waiting in the school or quietly walking around when you come in. You may have been watching the group ride with the previous candidate. If this is the case make sure that you have learnt each rider's name. It is far better to call your riders personally, by name, than say, for example, 'You on the bay horse', or continually call them by the wrong name. If you find it difficult to remember names, then take a note pad or small piece of card in your pocket and jot down the rider's names with some quick identifying feature, so that you can make a quick reference before naming them (e.g. Tina – bay horse, blue girth). If you have not been able to watch any of the lesson and are bad at remembering names, then certainly write them down and refer to them.

If it is a cold day then teach in your normal exam turnout but add a top coat:

- Shirt and tie.

- Fawn or beige breeches/jodhpurs.

- Long boots.

- Jacket.

- Hat (need not be fastened if this makes talking awkward; alternatively you could leave your hat on the side of the school, ready to pick up if needed).

- Gloves.

- Whip (like the hat, leave by the side of the school in case you need it).

- A tidy top coat or waterproof coat (especially if outside) which will fit comfortably over your jacket. It is essential as a teacher that you are warm, comfortable and dry.

If the riders are walking around when you move into the school to start your lesson, then call them into a line.

RIGHT: This instructor is neatly turned out for everyday teaching. She would have a riding hat, gloves and a whip close by in case she needed to ride a horse. More formal clothing would be appropriate for exam presentation (see text).

BELOW: Inappropriate presentation for teaching – casual and uninvolved with pupils.

- Introduce yourself and give a brief resume of what you are aiming to teach in your lesson. Explain the aim and the short-term goal of the session.

- Go to each rider and ask:

  (a) Their name.

  (b) Have they ridden the horse before?

  (c) Are they comfortable? Stirrups/girth?

- At this point make a superficial note of the tack. You should notice things like an over-tight throatlatch, a crooked noseband, and keepers not in place. If there are oversights such as these, then adjust them. Avoid saying, 'I'm going to check the tack', because if you miss something then you show that your tack check was not adequate!

2.1.2 Starting the lesson

When you teach any lesson, it is important to make an initial assessment of your riders. However, this should not be a period of the lesson where no instruction is given. It should be possible to move the ride around while you assess them but still introduce some comments about strengths and weaknesses of the riders. It is acceptable to work the ride either in closed order to start with, or in open order, as long as you explain clearly which you are choosing and why.

With fairly inexperienced riders it is often easier to assess them in closed order rather than allow riders you have never taught before to work in open order. Either method is acceptable; there is no right or wrong way.

You must show that you are in control, and as the teacher, able to make a balanced assessment of your ride, so that you can plan the next work.

In the first few minutes of the lesson, you want to assess the following:

- The basic competence and control of each rider.

- The basic position of each rider – how they sit, whether the balance is correct, and how they apply aids and influence the horse.

- Are they 'followers' or 'leaders'?

- Their basic confidence.

- The overall character of the rider (e.g. positive or timid).

Generally it is better to get the horses working forward and so loosen them up rather than start working on intricate figures and movements. Riders (clients) also feel more fulfilled if they can start riding positively from the start.

2.1.3 Assessing the rider's basic ability

As a result of the initial assessment working on both reins in walk and trot and perhaps seeing an individual canter, a plan can then be made of how to progress the lesson.

The first requirement of the teacher at Preliminary Teaching Test level is that you can:

- Assess the rider's correct basic position and be able to make corrections to help achieve a sound, basic position and one from which greater depth, effect and security can be developed.

- Maintain and assert basic control of a small number of riders on the flat and over ground poles and small jumps.

- Assess the rider's state of confidence and adjust work according to it.

- Work the rider in a safe and constructive way using appropriate exercises to develop balance, depth and effect in the riders' positions.

- Choose work which will not exhaust or demoralise the rider who may ride a horse only once a week, but will maintain enthusiasm and purpose in riders who want to aim higher.

Some individual work, either in open order or one at a time from the ride, would be appropriate to assess the confidence and effectiveness of each rider.

The **choice** of the latter content of the lesson will be affected by the initial assessment. The **aim** of the lesson will be formulated as a result of the assessment.

The assessment should allow the riders to settle and feel comfortable with themselves and the teacher. An early rapport between pupils and teacher should be apparent, so that an ideal learning environment is set up. This should help to dictate the outcome of the lesson and ensure that maximum benefit is achieved by the riders from the teacher.

The assessment should not be a period of time where the teacher only 'directs traffic', i.e. moves the ride around through a series of movements or changes of direction with no information forthcoming about the quality of the work shown, or basic help in how to improve what is being demonstrated. The assessment should be a balance between some work to indicate what level of competence the riders already have, with some ongoing help and corrections to improve what is being shown. The assessment should then be the forerunner of the main body of the lesson, which should be directly related to the weaknesses seen in the assessment.

2.1.4 Improving the rider's position

This must be a basic requirement for any lesson, whether class or individual, and to whatever level you ultimately aspire to teach. Riding a horse is all about the partnership of horse and rider, and the ability of the rider to convey clear and effective messages (aids) to the horse to create movement. The more in balance the rider can sit, the more they are able to follow the horse's movement and move with it, and the more easily the horse will be able to carry the rider's weight. The 'correct' rider position for work on the flat and jumping, is well documented in **The BHS Manual of Equitation**.

To be able to improve the rider's position, you must first be able to:

- Understand and recognise the correct, basic rider position for work on the flat and over fences.

- Recognise when the rider is out of balance and where the loss of balance comes from – e.g. if the lower leg is too far forward and not in line with shoulders and hips, this often puts the shoulders behind the vertical and the body behind the movement.

- Recognise when there are faults in the position and where the faults originate from – e.g. low and set hands may have their cause in tight shoulders, therefore the correction of the hands would come from the improvement of the shoulders.

- Recognise a lack of straightness in the saddle – e.g. seat slipping to inside or outside.

- Be able to recognise if the seat is straight but the shoulders are not level or if there is a twist in the upper body.

- Be able to recognise swiftly if the rider's stirrups are not level.

It is important that the rider accepts the corrections being made. Sometimes a rider may never have been told that his basic position is incorrect or that there is room for improvement. In this case tact is essential and riders must be encouraged to feel the difference in their effect, balance or control, when their position is improved. It is easy to neglect work on improving the basic rider position in an effort to satisfy the rider's desire to make progress into work that they see as more challenging (e.g. learning to canter and jump). The rider must be encouraged to understand that the improvement of the position is as intrinsic to developing skill as a horseman as practising scales are for a musician. Working on the depth, security and effect of the position will be an enduring part of every riding lesson to some degree or other.

There are many ways to work on improving the rider's position and the challenge to the teacher is to continue to provide a stimulating situation, whereby the rider feels motivated towards self-improvement.

Having identified the fault of each rider, it is helpful to highlight for each rider in the group where you see their strengths and weaknesses. If one or two areas are specified then the rider should be encouraged to focus on the particular fault and work to try and improve it. It is then important to choose work which will help the riders to achieve their goal.

The rider's position can be effectively improved by the following methods:

- Riding on the lunge under instruction. (This is covered in a separate chapter.)

- Riding without stirrups in all paces, depending on the rider's ability. There are very few occasions when work without stirrups, carried out in a structured way and taking into account such things as riding experience, rider fitness, rider confidence and comfort of the horse, does not contribute to rider improvement.

- Suppling exercises with and without stirrups, both on the move and in halt (depending on the difficulty of the exercise).

- Work with the reins in one hand.

- Riding bareback (without a saddle) to improve security, relaxation and feel of the horse's movement.

- Vaulting (gymnastic work on a trained lunge horse with a specialist vaulting instructor).

At Preliminary Teaching Test level you must be able to:

- Recognise the correct riding position on the flat and over fences.

- Compliment the riders on the correct aspects of their position.

- Refer to basic faults in the position and where they originate from.

- Choose a range of work and exercises whereby corrections can be made to the position and the rider is then able to feel the development of improvement. An outcome of success is therefore achieved which in itself is motivating to further achievement.

- Never neglect working on or improving the rider's position in the pursuit of attempting more demanding or exciting work.

- A poor, insecure or inadequate position ultimately will compromise the development of harmony and effect between horse and rider.

2.1.5 Improving aid application

The rider's ability to apply clear and coordinated aids (messages) to the horse, to establish control and enhance performance is based on the following:

- Clear understanding of what the 'aids' are.

- A good enough balance, through the development of a correct and secure position, that the aids can be clearly and consistently applied.

- A developing feel and awareness of the results that are forthcoming from the specific aids given.

It is therefore essential that teaching about the use and application of aids is intrinsically linked to the development of a good basic riding position on the flat and over fences, as discussed in the previous section. One cannot be achieved without the other. As the rider's position becomes more secure and balanced, so will the aid application become more consistent and clear and in turn the response of the horse should improve. The end product is a greater harmony between horse and rider as misunderstanding is reduced and fluency is improved.

As an aspiring Preliminary teacher you must have a clear understanding of:

- The natural aids (seat, legs, hands and voice).

- The artificial aids (whips, spurs, martingales).

As described in the last section you must be able to recognise a basic correct riding position on the flat and over fences. The work to improve aid application would then involve:

- Work without stirrups in all three paces (depending on riders' ability) to increase depth and security.

- Within the work without stirrups, frequent changes of pace (transitions) which test the rider's ability to (a) maintain balance; (b) apply clear aids while maintaining position to establish the transition.

- Repetition is essential to develop the rider's feel for when the transition is smooth, balanced, easy and fluent or rough and lacking harmony.

- Repetition enables the rider to practise the appropriate pressure or strength of the aid required, to create the result.

- Repetition enables the rider to practise varying the intensity of the aid, or where the relevant aid is applied and to what effect.

- Repetition ensures developing competence through practice.

- Repetition develops coordination.

- Changes of pace with and without stirrups ensure practice of aid application.

- Riding simple school movements, such as basic turns and circles, assists in the rider's ability to improve aid application and coordination.

The nature of riding as a sport dictates that the rider must develop awareness of the horse's body movements underneath him, as well as being aware of the functioning of his own body. Improved harmony between horse and rider comes as the rider 'fine tunes' his coordination and becomes able to apply aids appropriate to the sensitivity and attitude of the horse he is riding.

The Preliminary teacher must strive to teach the rider to be aware of the horse from the earliest stage and never use him as a 'bicycle' on which to learn. Naturally, beginner riders will lack balance and coordination, so they must always be mounted on a horse which will accept their inadequacies as novice riders and not be upset or anxious about them. A good teacher can limit the amount a horse is affected by a beginner rider, by the way he or she chooses work that is well within the range and ability of the novice. The horse should never have to 'put up with' bad riding, whether that is brought about by an unsympathetic attitude to the horse or by inadequacy in skill. As a Preliminary teacher it is essential that you develop a feeling for what the horse is dealing with, especially when he is helping you teach less competent riders to improve.

Exercises at halt (with an assistant to hold the horse), and in walk, trot and in some cases canter, will help riders to be more aware of how their hands and legs can work in harmony or in opposition to each other. Similarly arm and hand exercises will focus the rider's awareness on that part of their body.

As described in the previous section, exercises improve suppleness and therefore depth and security of the position; they also improve aid application and coordination.

It is important that the Preliminary teacher is able to explain clearly:

- The basis of being able to apply leg and hand aids comes from the ability of the rider to maintain security and balance in their seat.

- The leg aids should be thought of and applied a fraction before the corresponding hand or rein aids. With this in mind the novice rider is then always encouraged to think of riding the horse from leg to hand.

- Very rarely does a specific rein or leg aid act in isolation; this is why coordination is so vital.

- Most aids given to the horse to obtain a response involve a balance or coordination of each leg and each hand, applied together to produce one response.

2.1.6 Maintaining safety and development

Whether you are teaching novice riders, more competent riders, children or adults, it is essential that any lesson progresses and develops, but of paramount importance is that any lesson is safe.

By the very nature of riding, it can never be regarded as a sport without risk, if any such sport actually could exist. The teacher's job is to minimise the risk and to have made very clear judgments about how to develop the lesson, so that in the event of an unforeseen incident occurring, it is never as a result of the teacher's poor judgment of how the lesson should progress.

Several criteria can be listed which would help ensure safety is maintained:

- In class lessons the number of riders should be limited according to the facilities available, the standard of competence of the riders, and the level of experience of the teacher giving the lesson.

- The facilities which will be used for the lesson are well maintained (e.g. door or gate of school/arena – or field gate if class taking place in a paddock – must be in working order so that it can be closed while the lesson is in progress).

- The class of riders should all mount together in a controlled and monitored way:

  (a) preferably inside the school or arena where the lesson will subsequently take place;

  (b) with all the horses in a straight line with space between them;

(c) less experienced riders should be supervised during the mounting procedure.

- Wherever possible riders in a class lesson should be of similar standard.

- Generally, progress should be dictated by the least competent rider in the group rather than the most competent.

- If in doubt as to the suitability of an exercise for the ride, don't use it.

- If choosing to progress into an area of more difficult work, make sure that:

  (a) there has been clear explanation of the work or exercise;

  (b) the aids and procedure have been clearly outlined;

  (c) if necessary, a demonstration has been given;

  (d) the riders have confidence in your judgment to proceed with the work.

- At all times, whether working in open order, or especially when in closed order in a ride, be aware of the distance between one horse and another – this is essential.

- 'Safe' distance depends on a number of factors. In general in closed order, half a horse's length or one horse's length is appropriate. In 'open order' the term speaks for itself. There will be instances when horses are closer (e.g. when passing another rider on the inner track). In these instances if the rider is not experienced enough to use sufficient judgment then the teacher should be quick to advise. Awareness of a horse's tension and anxiety, and the possible reaction resulting, are the teacher's responsibility.

The remit of this book is not to list or attempt to highlight all the aspects of teaching which might relate to safety. Safety is a subject which the teacher of any sport, at any level, must feel passionately about. However, good awareness of safety develops through training and experience. Teachers must not become so anxious about safety that:

- They become defensive in their teaching and so lack progression, and they fail to actually teach their riders to make improvements.

- Over-sensitise their pupils to the issue of safety, so that they instil anxiety in their riders, which in itself inhibits development and creates a potentially unsafe environment.

As a Preliminary teacher you will develop a good sense of safety awareness if:

- You **NEVER** assume knowledge. Even if a rider tells you he can canter or jump, you must always make your own assessment of a rider and progress the work based on **YOUR** judgment of him.

- You **NEVER** pressurise a rider into attempting something that he tells you he cannot do or does not want to do.

- You **ALWAYS** concentrate on your riders, whether class or individual, and are not distracted by, say, a friend who comes to chat to you, your mobile phone or whatever is going on in the next field/arena or outside.

- You are aware of outside influences which might disrupt your lesson and take action accordingly (e.g. if a very windy day is making the horses more spooky, consider reducing the pace and complexity of the lesson).

- You try never to take your horses (or riders you teach often) for granted, thinking that you know what they can or can't do and how the horses 'always' go.

- Each day is different, every lesson must have an assessment so that irrespective of what you have planned to teach, you ultimately choose or adapt your work to accommodate the assessment on that day.

Development of work is essential to maintain enthusiasm and motivate riders towards further achievement. However, as previously described, repetition is also essential to establish secure foundations from which development is assured and easier.

Particularly for the beginner or novice rider, repetition of basic work will probably form the large percentage of any lesson. The teacher's job is to find a range of exercises, movements and work which will provide the repetition for the riders, while introducing as much variety as you can to maintain enthusiasm.

If you are finding difficulty in thinking of ways to develop the work without taxing riders beyond their ability, then try to watch other teachers to give you some ideas on a variety of exercises or work to use for different levels of rider.

2.1.7 Correct use of equipment

'Equipment' for a riding lesson may differently be classified as the horse, the tack for the horse, and the 'props', such as poles, jumps etc. In this section I am going to make some brief reference to the horse but concentrate more on inanimate equipment.

The **horse/pony** should ideally be appropriate to the level of rider being taught. If a beginner rider is mounted on a horse/pony which is perhaps more suited to a rider with some experience and ability, then a potentially dangerous situation may be promoted. As described under the last heading, awareness is paramount with regard to safety. If a rider is deliberately 'over-horsed' then the teacher is not showing due regard for safety. If a rider is unwittingly mounted on too difficult a ride for his level, then the assessment by the teacher should quickly highlight the fault. Therefore, one way or another, the rider should be remounted on a horse more appropriate to his level of expertise.

The Preliminary teacher **MUST** be capable of checking tack both on and off the horse and be confident about the following:

- You must be able to check that tack is in a safe and well-maintained state of repair for use by a rider and for the comfort of the horse.

- You must be able to fit tack safely and in such a way that the horse is comfortable. In particular the saddle should sit the rider in a way that you are able to teach a good basic position (flat or jumping) correctly. (If the saddle slopes backwards without the rider, then it is difficult to teach the rider to sit in a good position because the saddle is disadvantaging him.)

- You must be able to check the girth and stirrups of your riders, and offer advice on how to tighten or slacken the girth and adjust their stirrups.

- You must be able to look at riders from in front and behind and recognise when their stirrups are unlevel or they are sitting crooked in the saddle.

- When taking a lesson you must be able to notice, at a glance, if straps on bridles are not secure in keepers, if nosebands are crooked or too tight/slack.

- After a period of riding in you should encourage riders to check their girths (help them if necessary) as they may have slackened off while working in.

- In general terms, beginner and novice riders will find it easiest to learn to ride in a well-fitted general-purpose type saddle which allows them a little scope for developing a basic position and balance.

- Beginner and novice riders should always learn to ride with the horse in a snaffle bridle, requiring the rider to have to manage only one rein in each hand.

When using equipment in the school it is important that it is:

- Easily available when you want it, so that you do not have to leave the ride unattended to access it.

- In a safe, visible position if stored in the school, where it cannot cause a hazard in itself. Jump stands and poles can be safely stored in a neat pile on a threequarter line in the school. If stored in corners they should not be in a position to inhibit good use of the corners or where injury could occur by close contact. A small jump store with access directly into the school is ideal.

- Easy to handle and put in place, so that you or any assistants you might have can utilise it conveniently.

Equipment neatly stacked in centre of school and for use as needed in a lesson.

- Preferably made of materials which are light and need minimal maintenance. (Plastic jump stands, light poles and plastic cups are ideal.)

When jumps are actually in use, it is good policy:

- Never to jump fences with ground lines on the wrong side of the fence, i.e. on the opposite side to the line of approach or take-off .

- Never to jump fences with cups in the wings which do not hold a pole. (It is less dangerous if the cups are plastic as injury would be less likely, but if you adopt one policy then you will not need to remember that you can jump with plastic cups free but not with metal cups.)

- Always to jump fences with the lower part of a spread fence on the take-off side.

With other equipment such as cones, blocks or other obstacles:

- Always explain why you are using the equipment and what is expected of the rider.

- If in doubt, demonstrate on foot if not on a horse (e.g. bending in and out of cones).

- Do not assume that riders (or horses) will have seen the equipment before; introduce it slowly if necessary to gain the confidence of horses and riders.

- Keep them tidily stacked in one area when not in use. (Ideally place them in a corner or in an area off the track in the school.)

- Stacked jump stands should have their cups either detached or turned to face inwards.

2.1.8 Teaching the rider/horse partnership

The importance of teaching riding as a partnership between horse and rider cannot be overstressed or emphasised often enough. Whilst a beginner or inexperienced rider at any level must on many occasions have to concentrate hard on new areas of knowledge and application (e.g. how to sit on the horse, where to apply legs or hands) it is the teacher's responsibility to ensure that this learning is never at the expense of the horse. Teaching riding is always about teaching the rider to feel, understand and harmonise with the horse.

As a Preliminary teacher it will be important to emphasise with young or inexperienced pupils the need to:

- Handle the horse firmly and always consistently, so that the horse takes the authority from the rider both unmounted and mounted.

- Ask for help in leading, adjusting stirrups or girths and when mounting if necessary.

- Recognise that the horse is a living, breathing, thinking creature, with (at times) a mind of his own if he does not receive clear information from the rider.

- Recognise that the horse can be affected by things that frighten him or excite him, just as we are.

- Recognise that it is impossible to learn to ride without taking into account the way the horse thinks. Therefore developing awareness and feeling for the horse is a fundamental part of improving skills as a rider.

Within any lesson the progress of work may be dependent on this harmony and empathy between horse and rider. This must become clear to riders especially in a class lesson. Perhaps a rider in a weekly class lesson has cantered during one session, on a subsequent lesson they may be mounted on a horse that they do not find so easy to control, cantering in this instance would not be a well chosen exercise. Riders must be encouraged to realise that this is not a reflection of their lack of ability, but that progress with one horse may be more evident than on another which is a more difficult ride. Bearing this in mind, it is the teacher's responsibility:

- To choose work appropriate to how horses and riders are performing 'today' as a result of assessment (as described).

- Not to be pressurised by riders demanding that they, for example, canter or jump because they 'did so last week'.

- To gauge the level of work and exercises chosen with constant regard to many different variables which include: horse behaviour, outside influences, rider effort and achievement and any other circumstances arising on the day.

Sometimes if harmony between horse and rider is good then progress may be faster than anticipated. When such a circumstance exists, then progress positively to a satisfying development. When learning to ride, the committed rider will soon accept that progress can be very swift sometimes and then painfully slow at other times. This can be regarded as one of the challenges of the sport.

Occasionally a 'partnership' between horse and rider is not satisfactory. This is less common with riding school horses, because they tend to learn to accept many different rider abilities and attitudes and stay fairly level about the differences. Some sensitive horses, unused to being ridden by different riders, sometimes have a problem adapting. In this case the teacher may need to change riders to achieve better compatibility. This should not deteriorate into a situation where the rider always chooses the easiest and most popular horse. There must be a policy where riders are trained to recognise and accept the value of riding a wide variety of different types, which should further their riding abilities and help them develop a partnership with any horse. This is particularly useful for people sitting the various BHS exams where they will be required to ride several horses on their exam day, both on the flat and over fences.

2.1.9 Dealing with problems during a lesson

When teaching riding remember you are dealing with two living beings, one human and one horse, or in the case of a class lesson, several humans on several horses. It is impossible to produce a predictable situation on every occasion.

As previously described you will have taken every precaution to ensure that the lesson progresses safely, with regard for the welfare of the horses and the gradual development of the rider's work. It is important that you are prepared for unexpected situations and have some idea of how to deal with problems which may arise.

Problems may arise due to:

- Inclement weather (cold, wind or rain, indoors or outside, can cause anxiety in horses).

- Riders losing confidence and conveying their nervousness to the horse.

- Horse(s) making their own decisions and the rider then losing control.

- Even in the best organised lesson sometimes riders lose balance and fall off.

Many other situations may arise whereby a problem is perceived. Any deviation from the intended lesson plan may be construed as a problem. In reality the teacher's role is to monitor the ongoing lesson and through awareness try to avoid a problem. By adapting the progress of the lesson you may be able to prevent a greater problem from developing.

General guidelines for dealing with problems might be:

- If a horse misbehaves (bucks or spooks) bring the rest of the ride to walk or halt as swiftly as you can without panic.

- Similarly if a rider falls off, bring the rest of the ride to halt as soon as possible.

- More competent riders who ride in open order should be taught to stay out of the way of any rider experiencing problems with his horse. If in doubt, they should come down to a slower pace or halt until the rider is back in control.

- Concentrate on helping the rider in the most difficulty.

- Stay calm in your voice (irrespective of how tense the situation might seem!) but nevertheless assert confidence and authority. You can sometimes help to 'talk the horse down to calmness' even if the rider is anxious and not coping.

- Assess the reason for the problem and adjust the lesson accordingly.

- If necessary, change a rider who is in difficulty onto an easier horse, or onto a horse on which he feels more confident.

- In general, make the aim of the lesson less demanding, even return to an area of work where confidence in the riders is strong.

- Reassess the lesson afterwards to review whether the problem could have been avoided by a different procedure.

- In a future lesson avoid the circumstances which precipitated the problem.

Do not become anticipatory or nervous about problems developing. Minor incidents, and occasionally major incidents, are an integral part of teaching riding and your ability to deal with problems practically and confidently, if and when they arise, is part of your development as a competent teacher.

2.2 The Theory of Teaching

SECTION 2.2 COVERS ASPECTS of the theory of teaching. This section will be examined in a group discussion of up to six candidates. Questions will first be directed at individuals and then the subject should be opened up for open contribution from all participants. The examiner is seeking your knowledge and opinions on teaching various different types of riders (children, adults, beginners, more competent riders) in a variety of situations.

2.2.1 Value of various types of lesson

In discussing various types of lesson, you should feel happy to talk about the advantages and disadvantages of:

- Lead rein lessons for beginners (children or adults).

- Lunge lessons for beginners (children or adults).

- Individual lead rein or class lead rein lessons.

- Class lessons.

- Private lessons.

- Teaching groups or individuals on hacks or rides in the country.

- Stable management lessons (practical or theory).

- Jumping lessons.

- Lessons in a jumping paddock or open field.

- Two or three lessons going on in the same arena or school.

You might be expected to discuss:

- At what stage of the novice rider's experience would you introduce hacking out?

- When you would introduce some jumping position work and the introduction of ground poles.

- The effort involved for rider, horse and instructor in a private lesson compared to a class lesson.

- What sort of person may be better suited to private lessons as opposed to class lessons, and vice versa.

- The numbers of riders per lesson.

- Whether the number would vary if riders were beginners or more experienced.

2.2.2 Rider fitness and confidence

It is important to remember that riding is a sport. Learning a sport requires a degree of physical effort and it is not sufficient to suggest that the horse does the carrying of the rider! Children are less fit than they used to be: they walk to school less, do less compulsory sport at school, watch a fair amount of TV and eat more convenience foods.

As a riding instructor you have a responsibility to your pupils and the horses they ride, to encourage riders to make an effort to maintain a basic level of fitness if they are going to ride easily, enjoy the sport and develop their skill.

These days more and more children and adults are overweight. This is an issue which is sensitive and you must be very careful if advising someone that their size may inhibit their riding ability. The most effective way to address this, is to encourage the person themselves to recognise that someone who is fairly fit and not carrying too much excess weight will probably end up making swifter progress than an unfit, overweight person.

Confidence can be fragile and it can also be radically altered in one incident involving a bad experience. It is important that the teacher recognises the fragility of confidence, particularly in some people more than others.

Confidence breeds more confidence, similarly a loss of nerve can have a spiralling downward effect on a person's confidence.

It is a huge responsibility of the teacher to make sure that existing confidence is nurtured and enhanced and a lack of confidence is recognised and nursed along. In this way confidence should be developed rather than destroyed.

The teacher must never take the rider's confidence for granted, or assume that because the rider achieved something a week ago, it will be automatic this week.

Confidence can be enhanced by a caring but firm teacher. It can just as easily be destroyed by an anxious teacher who fails to instil confidence in his/her pupil. It can also be crushed by a bullying attitude from the teacher, pressurising the pupil into work that they do not feel comfortable in.

Developing the rider's confidence through tactful but firm encouragement, so that they achieve beyond their expectations, can be one of the most satisfying situations a teacher can enjoy.

The role of the Preliminary teacher is to be able to recognise confidence or a lack of it in their individuals or classes of riders.

Signs of an over-confident rider can be:

- Saying how much they can do. (Usually with a novice rider the benchmark is that they can 'gallop' and 'jump four foot'!)

- Asking or insisting that they are leading file if the class is working as a ride.

- Wanting to canter more, jump higher, etc. given any opportunity because they believe they are so very good,

- Talking incessantly about how much they've done or are about to do!

- Talking non-stop.

A rider lacking confidence may:

- Also talk a lot (more than usual) to mask their anxiety.

- On the other hand, be rather silent and withdrawn.

- Continually tell you that they don't want to or can't do something.

- Ask not to canter, jump or whatever they feel like avoiding.

- Show some tension or stiffness in the upper body or gripping up with the lower leg.

- Be reluctant to carry out anything that they perceive as difficult (e.g. work without stirrups).

- Show a preference for one or two 'favourite horses'.

Tact and confidence in your own authority are essential ingredients in dealing with opinionated riders who may not respond to instruction due to their own state of confidence.

2.2.3 Length of lesson and choice of work

The length of a lesson in a commercial riding school will often be dictated by the policy of the establishment. When dealing with clients it is usual to be able to quote them a specific price for a lesson which will be of a designated time span. When teaching private lessons with competition riders, or individuals working on one specific area of development, the approach may be different. With these riders often the aim of the lesson is more important than the exact time span of the lesson. When the aim is achieved then the lesson concludes. Sometimes this may take longer than expected, and at other times it might be a short lesson but with high achievement. Riders who ride only once a week in a riding school are usually anxious to enjoy every moment of the lesson and may be disappointed if a lesson scheduled to run for one hour is concluded in 50 minutes. Conversely if a lesson of an hour's duration over-runs by 10 minutes, it may disrupt the school's schedule for the rest of the day, which is unprofessional.

A generally acceptable policy in many commercial establishments would be as follows:

- Private lessons (lead rein or lunge) for beginner or novice riders – minimum of 30 minutes, maximum of 45 minutes. (See also section 2.2.6.)

- Class lessons (maximum of eight riders) – minimum of 45 minutes, maximum of 60 minutes.

- Shared private lessons (two or sometimes three riders) will pay a little more than a full class lesson. Duration of the lesson could be a minimum of 30 minutes and a maximum of 60 minutes.

Occasionally, if establishments take very small children just to 'sit on a pony,' these may be led around for 15 to 20 minutes. Small children have a very short attention span and a relevant question for the Preliminary teacher to consider might be, 'At what age can a small child usefully start to have riding lessons of a formal nature?'

The following considerations could be:

- The physical stature of a very small child, in being able actually to influence the pony other than just being led about.

- The concentration of the child and their ability to take in taught information.

- The confidence of the child.

It is arguable whether a child under the age of four can be taught on a regular basis and make some consistent progress. Some establishments have a policy of not accepting children for lessons under the age of four, five or six. Most centres take them from the age of seven, if not before. Problems can arise when there are two or more children from one family and the younger sibling wants to carry on the same activity as his older brother or sister.

The choice of work, as stated so many times throughout this book, will always be dictated to some degree by assessment, and perhaps on some past knowledge of the rider. A beginner or rider attending for his first ever riding lesson may have no prior knowledge of riding at all. It is then necessary to 'start from scratch'. As a teacher it is essential that you are continually able to recall what it is like to know nothing about the activity your pupil is attempting. Your ability as a teacher is greatly enhanced if you can communicate the smallest detail to your pupils in everything they are to learn.

Be careful particularly with beginner or novice riders not to try to progress too quickly. Novice riders will gain far more confidence if they feel very secure in the work they are doing and show a desire to try something more difficult, rather than feel pressurised into trying something they do not feel very brave about.

In general the work should develop as follows:

- Always pay attention to detail in the way riders mount. Mounting safely is in the best interests of the rider and the well-being of the horse.

- Begin the lesson with a simple plan of warming up both horse and rider so that riders feel comfortable in their stirrups and are able to relax and begin to focus on their riding.

- Some simple walk, and possibly rising trot work may be appropriate on both reins.

- The aim of the first ten or fifteen minutes should be to recap on the previous week's work, to make sure that the rider(s) is working at the same level as he finished in the last lesson. For many reasons previously discussed, this may not automatically be the case.

- Depending on the first ten or fifteen minutes' work, then choose an area of work that you feel you will be able to fulfil in the next forty minutes.

- Always be prepared to change plan within your lesson:

  (a) to maintain the confidence of the riders;

  (b) to maintain the riders' understanding of the work;

  (c) to ensure that the riders feel they are making progress;

  (d) to maintain the safety of the lesson if outside influences are causing a problem (e.g. horses misbehaving in windy weather).

To the best of your ability always:

- Finish on a good note.

- Do not start something new in the last ten minutes of a lesson; if it proves difficult to teach or achieve progress with, you will not have time to sort out the problems.

- Always sum up your lesson by recapping on the work covered to ensure understanding.

- Work your riders within their capability (both mentally and physically) so that they leave feeling positive, not exhausted or deflated.

Sometimes if you are taking a class lesson where riders are a little uneven in their standard, you may have to choose work of a varying degree of difficulty to challenge each rider equally.

2.2.4 Escorting hacks or instructional rides

The Preliminary teacher should ideally have had some experience of assisting the escorting of hacks or instructional rides in the countryside.

As a holder of BHS Horse Knowledge and Riding Stage 2 you will hold your Riding and Road Safety Test. You must have a clear understanding of safety aspects of riding on the road, and particularly have knowledge of what the UK Highway Code states with regard to horses on the public highway.

You can expect questions on any of the following subjects in the oral discussion:

- How many riders would be safe to escort on the road in a group?

- What kind of supervision would there be (e.g. number of escorts and of what competence)?

- How would the ride be mounted prior to leaving the yard?

- Procedure for checking girths and stirrups.

- Practical equipment which would be wise to take with you on the hack.

- How the group would be organised with regard to position of the escort(s).

- How the route would be chosen, with what considerations in mind (e.g. busy roads, quiet country lanes, bridlepaths, open moorland or similar).

• How long a ride would be planned.

There may be questions on the procedure in the event of an accident on the road. This discussion should always involve reference to the action to be taken on return to the yard, with regard to the reporting and recording of the accident with possible follow-up to the incident.

Discussion may involve procedure over bridlepaths or open spaces such as moorland:

■ What paces might be chosen and why?

■ What structure might the ride take (e.g. one behind the other)?

■ The practicality of including small jumps during the ride.

If riding on the road:

■ What precautions should be taken with regard to visibility to other road users. (reflective clothing / fluorescent clothing / for horse/rider)?

■ Procedure for acknowledging courteous drivers.

■ How to manage if you need to dismount, help another rider or ride and lead another horse.

And on hacking in general:

■ What standard should the riders be before you introduce them to hacking out?

■ What are the advantages and disadvantages of hacking out, to horse? and rider?

If a ride is to be instructional, you should have ideas about how much information you would give before leaving the ride and what this might include.

■ What information would you be able to give during the hack?

You must understand the basic rules and regulations with regard to conduct and procedure on footpaths (no riding of horses) and bridlepaths.

You should know that maintaining and developing bridleways is one of the many roles of the British Horse Society. It has a network of Bridleways Officers throughout the whole country to advise and action any poorly maintained or abandoned bridlepaths.

In the worst scenario you must be able to discuss a procedure for dealing with a rider who falls off and may not be well enough to ride home independently. In this case you must be able to discuss the options for what you might do, including seeking support and assistance to deal with the crisis.

You may have to discuss the importance of an assessment of riding skill from a client before sending them out on a hack. **NEVER TAKE FOR GRANTED WHAT IS SAID.** Always make your own assessment and decide on your ride route as a result of assessing rider competence on that day. Always choose a ride route well within the competence of your least competent rider.

Hacking out can develop a rider substantially, as long as their confidence is maintained. Observation of the rider's 'nerve' and confidence is essential, by the escort, in dictating the smooth passage of a ride out or hack. Riders learn to be more independent – it is vital that they give the horse clear information, so that the influence they develop is their own, and gradually the horse becomes more respectful and listens to the rider.

2.2.5 Lesson structure and content

In discussion you may be asked about planning a lesson, the structure of a lesson and its content. The plan for a lesson will depend on some information which you need to have beforehand:

- Individual or class?

- If a class lesson, how many riders?

- Are the riders of similar age and ability, or mixed ages and standard?

- Where will the lesson take place?

- Have you taught the group or individual before (this will give you prior knowledge)?

- How long is the lesson to be?

- Is the lesson to be a specific lesson (e.g. jump lesson, lunge lesson)?

Going into a lesson with some ideas about what work might be appropriate for the ride is good planning. The full development of the lesson would then be decided on by the assessment of the riders in the first part of the lesson.

A typical lesson structure could be itemised as:

- Introduction of yourself to your pupil(s) and briefly finding out about them and their horse(s).

- Initial working in / warming up to include an assessment of your rider(s).

- As a result of the assessment, choosing work appropriate to developing the rider's ability in an area which you decide (in agreement with your pupil/s)) is going to help them most.

- As the lesson progresses, making continuous reassessment of how the work is helping the rider(s).

- As the lesson draws to a conclusion, making sure that you finish on a positive note.

- Before leaving your rider(s) checking to make sure they understand the lesson and can ask any questions that they want to about the work.

The content of the lesson:

- Should generally be aimed at the rider who is least competent, so that he is not overfaced by work too difficult for him.

- Riders of greater ability should be taxed in a way that challenges them without intimidating the less able riders (e.g. competent riders carry out an exercise without stirrups, while more novice riders keep their stirrups for that exercise).

Lesson length may often be dictated by the time allocations of class or private lessons in a commercial riding school. Private lessons may vary between 30 minutes (often for lead rein or lunge lessons) and 60 minutes, with often 40 or 45 minutes being a favoured period. Class lessons would normally be of one hour's duration with sometimes a longer period allocated for jumping sessions with a large group.

You should be able to decide what work could be appropriate to fill a 30 minute lesson, for example, for a class of four riders who can walk, trot and canter.

You should be able to discuss exercises and movements which would be appropriate to teach beginner or fairly novice riders (e.g. simple turns, large circles, diagonals in trot), similarly discuss work that would be more demanding for more able riders (e.g. smaller circles, turns on the forehand, leg yielding).

You may be asked to talk about the way a simple jumping lesson would be built up. This should include:

- How and when to introduce 'jumping position' or 'the light seat'.

- When to introduce poles and how to use them.

- Clear understanding of the working distances for:

  (a) trotting poles;

  (b) a placing pole in front of a small jump with a trot approach;

  (c) two small jumps with one non-jumping stride in between the two elements, with a trot approach;

  (d) a double of two fences ridden from canter with one non-jumping stride between the jumps.

You should be able to talk about the basic shape and construction of small jumps.

- When and why to use trotting poles.

- When to use a cross-pole.

- When to use a small vertical or upright fence.

- When and why to use a 'ground line'.

- When and why to use a placing pole in front of a fence.

- When to use a filler in a jump, and how to introduce it to a rider who has jumped only poles to date.

The content of a lesson should always be dictated to some degree by how the riders are working on the particular day and how their horses are going for them.

2.2.6 Lunge and lead rein lessons

In the theory discussion on teaching, you may be asked to compare the differences in teaching a beginner or fairly novice rider on the lead rein or on the lunge. You should be able to talk about the following:

- The labour intensity of one instructor giving lunge lessons (private, one to one).

- The demand that lungeing puts on either the horse or pony.

- The comparative demand that lungeing makes on space available for teaching.

- The benefits of lungeing to a rider.

- The benefits of using a lead rein lesson.

- The possible disadvantages of both these methods of teaching beginners.

For lungeing, the horse must be reliable and secure in his balance on the circle before he can cope with a rider. A good, consistent, reliable lunge horse is a valuable commodity and must be nurtured and his quality of work maintained.

As a Preliminary teacher you must be capable of lungeing a horse competently and effectively, so that it is possible to teach a helpful lesson on a horse that is moving forward adequately.

The length of a lunge lesson, to be commercially viable, would be between 30 and 45 minutes. Taking into account preparation for, and mounting time, which might take 10 to 15 minutes with a beginner or nervous rider, this would allow 15 to 30 minutes actual riding time. As lungeing a rider is demanding for any horse, this factor would also be considered in deciding the period of riding time. The lesson will involve some stopping, starting, changing direction and possible exercises at the halt, so ultimately 15 to 25 minutes is likely to be movement out on the lunge. All the other areas mentioned, apart from the actual riding, are essential and very valuable to the developing rider.

When giving a lead rein lesson, the quality of the forwardness of the basic walk and trot is also very relevant so that the rider becomes aware from the outset of the need for gaits that actually are purposeful and forward. Leading the horse/pony well is a prerequisite to being able to teach a competent lead rein lesson.

Attention to detail is essential so that the quality of teaching and learning is high.

You should be familiar with exercises which help to develop the work and yet are suitable for more novice or perhaps nervous people.

Some exercises are more appropriately carried out at a standstill, with someone holding the horse's head. The rider can then practise the exercise, safe in the knowledge that the horse will not move or become unsettled. Any of the following exercises would be appropriate for beginner or novice riders:

- Arm circling (one at a time, backwards).

- Lower leg swinging from the knee down (one at a time or both together).

- Draw legs (one or both) up the saddle in front of the rider, maintaining balance and position. With an energetic push, stretch legs down the horse's side.

- Shoulder shrugging.

Bending down to touch the toe – a useful exercise for adults and children. The horse/pony must always be held for this exercise, which is carried out at halt.

Bending down to touch the other toe. The lower leg has lost position.

Carried out at a standstill with someone holding the horse:

- 'Scissors' (needs a demonstration).

- 'Half scissors' (easier than full scissors).

- 'Around the world.'

- Leaning down to touch the toe on the near side and then on the off side.

Anything which enhances the flexibility of the rider, improves their feel and coordination and develops their independence is of great benefit to the novice rider.

Children can be encouraged to use the exercises to help them develop quickness and efficiency. Exercises including mounting and dismounting from the near and off sides will also improve confidence and a sense of self-survival.

Continuous assessment of the developing position is easy from the lunge or lead rein, but you must be aware that some faults are not always easy to recognise (e.g. sitting to the outside of the horse on a circle). Some faults may become well established and therefore more difficult to eradicate.

As a teacher you must think of ways to tempt your pupils to apply themselves to self-improvement.

2.2.7 Dealing with problems during a lesson

In the discussion you may be asked about any area of a lesson, class or individual where problems may arise. You should have some ideas on how to avoid problems occurring and how to deal with unforeseen incidents. By good planning, careful assessment and ongoing review of the lesson as it progresses, problems should be minimal. However, as discussed, the horse is a living animal and as such on occasions may have a mind of his own. Your ability as a Preliminary teacher must demonstrate a competence in both discussion and if necessary in the practical situation, to deal with any unexpected occurrence. The aim is to minimise the effect of the incident and to maintain the confidence of your pupil(s) to the best of your ability.

Horses can be upset or unsettled by:

- Unexpected loud noises.

- Unexpected sudden movement.

- Noise and movement, the cause of which cannot be seen.

- Other horses misbehaving.

- Extreme weather conditions (high wind; driving rain; sharp, cold, frosty weather).

Some horses may react unexpectedly when:

- The rider loses balance in the saddle, slips sideways or backwards and grabs at the horse.

- If presented in an unbalanced or very crooked approach to a jump.

- If the rider becomes tense and anxious and tightens up, restricting the horse's ability to go forward.

- If any equipment loosens and flaps (e.g. the rider loses a stirrup and the stirrup bangs against the horse's side; or the rider loses the reins and they flap around the horse's neck and face).

- If one horse is left isolated in a part of the school or out in an open area where the other horses have left him (e.g. all riders at one end of the school having jumped a fence or grid, one rider is left still to come through the exercise).

Many of the above instances can be avoided through forethought on the part of the teacher. Calmness in dealing with a problem is essential. A calm voice and attitude can repair a potentially anxious moment, whereas tension in the teacher's voice and an over-reaction to the incident can make the situation considerably worse.

When dealing with problems:

- Always reduce the pace of the rest of the ride or stop the work altogether.

- Give as much attention to the person experiencing difficulty as possible without compromising the safety of the rest of the ride.

- When the problem has been resolved, work gradually back to the area of difficulty by progressively rebuilding the work up towards the problem.

- If necessary, stop short of revisiting the area which promoted the problem, unless you are quite sure that the criteria which prompted the problem have been eradicated.

- Always discuss the problem with the rider; make sure that they are aware of what happened and why. It is vital that they feel in control of the outcome of dealing with the problem, otherwise they may worry about being in the same situation on a future occasion. They must feel that with your help they will be able to deal with the problem themselves.

2.2.8 Accident procedure

In the unfortunate event that an accident occurs, the teacher must be swift in his ability to deal with it, with confidence and reassurance to those involved.

Accidents occurring in the stable yard or stable which involve a person who is not mounted at the time:

- Always go to the injured person immediately.

- Assess the situation.

- Call for assistance if possible.

- Remove any horse(s) in close proximity if at all possible.

- Reassure the person(s) involved.

- Administer first aid as appropriate. Usually this should involve reassurance, keeping the person still, making him as comfortable mentally and physically as possible, and deciding on the next course of action through assessment of the situation.

- If in any doubt, always seek medical or paramedical support.

- In minor incidents, reassurance is the most essential commodity, and then staying with the person until he dictates his state of recovery.

Dealing with an accident in a lesson taking place in an indoor or outdoor school (more often than not this will involve a rider falling from their horse):

- Immediately halt the rest of the ride.

- Go swiftly to the person on the ground.

- Assess the seriousness of the fall, and if necessary send for help.

- Encourage the person to stay still and not be in a hurry to get up.

- Reassure him calmly.

- If necessary, and if someone is capable within the ride, ask them to catch the loose horse; if this is not appropriate wait until help comes.

- Make a decision as to:

  (a) whether the rider can continue if only a minor incident;

  (b) whether the rider should sit out the rest of the lesson, resting quietly with someone with them;

  (c) whether the rider should be accompanied back to the yard with support;

  (d) whether medical or paramedical support is needed as soon as possible at the site.

These decisions must be made taking into account the circumstances of each and every incident.

If an accident occurs while a rider is out on a country ride or hack:

- All the above criteria apply, but extra consideration must be given to the safety of the possibly injured person if there is a risk of traffic around.

If a rider falls off on the road:

- Dismount, give your horse to your assistant escort or the next most competent person in the ride.

- Go to the injured person. Give reassurance.

- Halt the ride off the road, in a gateway or on a grass verge if possible.

- Send your two most competent riders to warn oncoming traffic (on either side) of the incident. They should stay in sight of the rest of the ride so that the horses are not unsettled unnecessarily.

- Sometimes it may be possible to enlist the help of a driver or a pedestrian who may be willing to assist.

- If possible and necessary, use a mobile phone to summon help from the yard, and in the worst case scenario to call for medical or paramedical help.

Accidents occur even in the most efficiently and well-run lessons. It is unfortunately an innate part of the sport. In most cases the rider is uninjured or receives minimal bumps or bruises. The teacher's responsibility is to minimise the risk of accidents by:

- Choosing work appropriate to the level of riders.

- Progressing the lesson according to assessment and ongoing review.

- Listening to and liaising with riders to identify their level of confidence and attitude to working towards more challenging work.

- Maintaining an ongoing awareness of the horses' attitude and behaviour within any lesson.

After any incident or accident, on return to the yard a full and comprehensive record of the event must be made in the incident/accident book as soon as possible after the problem has been dealt with. This is covered with more emphasis in the next section.

2.2.9 Maintaining records

Recording information in any business is essential and reflects a well-run operation. It enables the owner, manager or person of seniority within the establishment to monitor all procedures and adapt them as and when necessary, based on evidence accumulated over a period of time. This evidence indicates trends and patterns of activity, which may need adjusting from time to time to maintain good practice. A good example would be an incident book in which any out of the ordinary occurrence is recorded. For example, a horse or pony who repeatedly appears in the book (irrespective of rider or instructor) for treading on people's feet, is either bossy and needs a period of discipline, or is being used for riders without sufficient ability or experience to handle him safely. The policy for use of this horse/pony needs adjusting or he needs retraining.

The Preliminary teacher should be able to talk about maintaining the records, which could be simply categorised in two sections:

1. Records maintained in the office relating to clients riding at the establishment

- There should be information recorded on every client who rides at the centre. This would be taken at their first booking at the school and would include: name, address, date of birth (mandatory if under 18), contact telephone number, next of kin and contact number if different from own, height, weight, any special information especially relevant to health which would be appropriate knowledge for the activity of riding (e.g. diabetic or epileptic).

- The day book, or diary, will record any bookings for lessons. Systems will be tailored to each establishment. They may record lessons booked for each instructor employed by the centre, or they may have a general booking system whereby instructors are allocated subsequently.

- Bookings and records may also be recorded electronically (on computers).

- Usually, some kind of daily list will be displayed so that all employees can see what their commitments are through the day; while visiting clients can identify which horse they have been allocated for their lesson.

The Preliminary teacher (although this is not his responsibility) should be aware that within a commercial establishment there is a legal obligation to display (probably in the office):

- A current registration of the business name.

- A health and safety policy (if the centre employs more than four people).

It is advisable to display:

- The certificate of insurance for public liability.

- The local authority licence.

- The BHS Approval plaque current for the year.

Also in the vicinity of the office it is advisable to have a notice board which gives information about the centre, what services it offers and a current price list. Any forthcoming activities (e.g. children's courses during the school holidays) should be posted up and the information should be current, interesting and regularly updated.

The incident or accident book should also be lodged in the office and must be completed as soon after an occurrence as is reasonably possible. The Preliminary teacher should always be able to refer to someone more senior in charge of the establishment at any time, when they are teaching. A qualified BHSAI (holder of the Preliminary Teaching Certificate, Stage 3 and having completed 500 hours teaching experience) may be conducting lessons in the absence of a more senior instructor. He or she must be aware that any incident/accident must be recorded and occurrences of a more serious nature requiring any visit to hospital are subject to possible reporting under the 'Reporting of Injuries, Diseases and Dangerous Occurrences Regulations' (RIDDOR).

2. Records maintained in the stable yard, relating to horses/ponies
These may include:

- A current list of horses/ponies in commercial use in the riding school (all those listed under the local authority riding school licence).

- Shoeing records – when each horse was last shod, needs trimming, reshoeing, etc.

- Veterinary records – when each horse was vaccinated (especially against tetanus).

- A list of livery horses and their belongings.

- A feedchart which is current and kept up to date for every horse/pony.

- Tack records, with particular reference to maintenance and repairs.

Records of things such as forage and bedding delivery may be in the yard or the office depending on the management system in place at the yard.

Each establishment will have a specific and to some degree individual policy for the following:

- Introducing a new client to the centre and dealing with him for his first lesson.

- Taking payment for lessons, including ideas for tempting riders to make a regular commitment to lessons.

- Advising clients on appropriate clothing and offering tactful help if clothing is unsafe or likely to be inadvisable for safe or comfortable riding.

- Allocation of horses/ponies.

- Discussing lesson options with clients (hacks, jumping, lunge lessons).

- Advice on riding hats or body protectors.

- Grading riders in lessons, according to ability or (in the case of children) age.

- Options for adult/children holiday courses or days.

2.2.10 Progressing lessons

Much reference has been made in many of the previous sections about the progression of lessons. The Preliminary teacher must demonstrate both practically and in discussion their clear understanding of when and how to progress lessons.

Progression of any lesson, whether private or class, must always be dictated by:

- Overall confidence of the rider(s) in the lesson.

- Clear understanding of the work already covered.

- Desire to want to progress and try more challenging work.

- Circumstances on that occasion, e.g. behaviour of horses/ponies, outside influences, fitness of riders.

- Competence and experience of the instructor.

Progression of lessons must **NEVER** be dictated by:

- The rider(s) demanding that they do something particular (e.g. canter or jump) **AGAINST** the better judgment of the instructor.

- The rider(s) insisting that the instructor last week promised that this week they could do something particular (e.g. canter or jump), again against the judgment of this week's instructor. This indicates a very clear necessity for there to be a good liaison between two instructors who teach the same group on consecutive weeks, so there is no risk of the rider(s) playing one instructor off against the other.

- Pressure from outside (e.g. parents) that the rider(s) must do 'whatever' this week because their friend/daughter is doing it!

It is essential that as a Preliminary teacher you develop sufficient self-confidence and authority in your own ability that you never progress a lesson against your better judgment or a 'gut feeling' that the rider(s) may not be able to cope. If you are in a position where that situation might be compromised, then you should seek the support or advice of a more senior instructor at the establishment.

It is important to remember that clients who ride for only one hour a week will progress much more slowly than those who ride four or five times a week. As a Preliminary teacher you probably ride regularly yourself, especially if you are working for your Stage 3 exam at the same time. Avoid comparing the weekly rider with your own aspirations – they are probably riding primarily for pleasure and enjoyment, whereas you may be driving yourself harder with a greater personal goal. It is essential that in your teaching you are able to identify with the lack of coordination and familiarity with the horse that is quite common to weekly riders, and allow them time to repeat work frequently to develop competence. The secret is to find various ways to repeat the same work.

That way the repetition is not boring, and the riders feel stimulated or challenged by the variety, without necessarily being stretched beyond their ability by staying within the same levels of work. It is important also to remember that the weekly rider will get tired more quickly, both physically and mentally. With that in mind, rest periods, during which riders can watch each other in a class lesson, can sometimes be beneficial.

Any lesson should have some broadly estimated plan (as previously described). From this loose plan, and as a result of assessment, the main body of the lesson can be formulated. This work should have an aim, a short-term goal, and a progression which could lead to a longer-term goal. For example, as a result of assessment the short-term goal for that lesson might be to introduce canter to a beginner rider who is ready to start to learn canter. The longer-term goal would be to develop the understanding of and ability to ride the canter, to a point where there is a good appreciation of the leading leg in canter and how to achieve it.

Any teacher's aim must always be to progress the lesson:

- With maximum regard for safety of the rider(s) at all times.

- With clear uptake of understanding.

- With awareness of the rider's physical and mental state.

- With maximum enjoyment of the lesson through involvement and commitment of the teacher to stimulate participation by the pupil(s).

- To encourage feedback from the pupil(s) which can help direct the progress of the lesson.

- To develop the lesson to a satisfactory conclusion.

- To reach a conclusion which leaves the pupil(s) with a constructive feeling to go home with, which should then act as motivation for the next lesson.

2.3 The Lunge Lesson

THIS SECTION LOOKS AT THE SPECIFIC REQUIREMENTS of a lunge lesson. Note that information and advice on lunge lesson length has already been discussed in section 2.2.6.

2.3.1 Suitability of the horse

Giving a lunge lesson is a specialist skill in its own right. It demands competence of the handler in lungeing effectively, and it then requires a horse with particular qualities to be a suitable ride for a lunge lesson.

The nature of the lesson is that the rider is mounted on a horse which is lunged, usually by the same person who is giving the lesson. The lesson is conducted with the horse working on a large and consistent circle of between 15 and 20 metres diameter.

Prior to commencing the lesson, the Preliminary teacher should work the horse in briefly before mounting the rider. This enables you to see how the horse behaves, what his way of going is like and how easy he is to control through your commands. It also loosens the horse and warms him up a little, so that he should be more comfortable both for himself and for the rider.

The horse should ideally have the following qualities:

- Be at least six years old, so that he is physically and mentally mature, as lungeing is both physically and mentally demanding.

- Have smooth, consistent, rhythmical paces, particularly in trot, which is likely to be utilised most.

- Make smooth and obedient transitions from one pace to another.

- Be calm and obedient to the teacher.

- Be equable and unflappable if anything unexpected happens (particularly for beginner or novice riders).

- Maintain a forward-going pace easily, without falling in or out on the circle.

The horse suitable for a more advanced level of pupil may:

- Have paces which have greater lift and movement than for the novice rider.

- Be a little more challenging in overall activity, requiring the rider to feel for balance and coordination.

- Should still be calm, obedient and reliable.

- Work easily on both reins.

The horse should be of an appropriate size for the rider. While a small rider may ride a horse which could be deemed too big for them, the opposite should not occur. A rider who is under-horsed will find it difficult to achieve balance and coordination, particularly on the lunge.

The horse should be well trained as a lunge horse and should have carried riders on the lunge before being used for a lunge lesson. A horse should be introduced to lunge work with a rider, using a student or member of staff at the establishment, before he should be used for paying clients.

The lunge horse should not be over-wide, particularly for a smaller, slighter rider. A fairly broad-backed horse, however, often gives a greater feeling of security for the rider, particularly the beginner or novice.

2.3.2 Lunge lesson equipment

The horse who is to be used for a lunge lesson to train the rider should wear the following equipment:

- Snaffle bridle.

- General-purpose or dressage saddle.

- Brushing boots, for protection, on all four legs.

- Well-fitting cavesson, fitted over the bridle, usually with the noseband removed.

- Side-reins.

- A neckstrap.

The teacher should then carry a lunge whip and rein. The lunge rein must be long enough for you to be able to lunge the horse on a comfortably large enough circle as previously described.

It is of vital importance that the horse wears well-fitted tack. For the rider, the saddle must be big enough to enable him to find a position and balance easily. When lungeing a rider it is also of great importance that the saddle will enable the rider to sit in the best possible position on the horse's back. If the saddle slopes backwards or forwards then it is very difficult for a rider to be able to achieve a correct, balanced position.

Usually a general-purpose saddle is more appropriate for a beginner or novice rider. They will find it easier to develop an as yet not established position in the non-specific scope of a general-purpose saddle. As the competence of the rider develops he may appreciate being lunged in a dressage saddle. The more specific nature of the specialist saddle can help a more experienced rider achieve greater depth and security in an already basically established seat.

The horse should be lunged from a well-fitted cavesson. Side-reins should be well fitted and used while the horse is actually on the move on the lunge. They should be clipped up out of use when leading the horse to and from the site where the lesson will take place.

The Preliminary teacher should demonstrate professional handling of the equipment at all times. The whip should be directed backwards under your arm while leading the horse in and out to the lesson. Throughout the lunge lesson it should be in use as required. It should not be put on the floor at any time. Should you drop the lunge whip by accident then either:

- Pick it up quietly and swiftly without taking your eyes off the horse and losing control, OR

- Leave it on the floor and stop the horse, then pick up the whip and resume.

When lungeing a horse either with or without the rider, it is wise to use gloves. It is very easy for a horse to pull unexpectedly and give you a nasty rope burn. Gloves will help protect from this. It is sensible to wear a riding hat (done up), particularly with a young or unpredictable horse. When giving a lunge lesson with a safe school horse, a hat may not be considered essential.

It is unwise to lunge a horse while wearing spurs. It is very easy to trip yourself up when wearing spurs, and this could create an added complication if you are lungeing a horse and it became frightened. As with riding the horse, safe footwear is essential when lungeing. Trainers or soft shoes are totally unacceptable.

2.3.3 Lunge lesson site and safety

In a commercial riding school, it is very likely that a beginner or novice lesson would be taken in an indoor school or on an outdoor all-weather surface. The footing underneath the horse is a major consideration when lungeing at any time but particularly when a rider is mounted on the horse.

Lungeing subjects the horse to additional stresses on his limbs, induced by working him continually on a relatively small circle. Working the horse on a consistent and good surface will minimise the effect of the stress.

The site for the lunge lesson should be considered with the following criteria taken into account:

- A minimum of 20m by 20m should be allowed. This will ensure that you have enough room to mount the rider safely and work the horse on a big enough circle with a little leeway around it.

- While it is possible that there may be other lessons going on in the same arena, the other instructors must take care not to encroach on the lunge lesson's space.

- If indoors, or in an outdoor enclosed school, it is better to employ one end of the school rather than the middle, so that the lunge horse is not in close contact with other horses on all sides.

- The ground surface should be as consistent and level as possible. Heavy or uneven ground will potentially lame a horse quickly.

- There should be as little outside distraction as possible. Particularly avoid a site where sudden or unexpected noises or movements might occur.

Safety considerations are essential in any lesson. There are one or two specific criteria for safety that perhaps apply only to lunge lessons. Points for safety could be listed as follows:

- As with all lessons, the rider must lead the horse safely (if necessary with supervision and assistance) to the lesson area.

- The horse should be briefly worked in without the rider to ensure that he is warmed up and will behave reliably for the rider.

- The horse should be worked in with and without side-reins.

- The rider must mount safely (with assistance if necessary).

- The side-reins **MUST** be undone for the rider to mount.

- Prior to the commencement of the lesson the side-reins should be reattached (from girth to bit).

- At all times the teacher must be aware of the way of going of the horse (e.g. not forward enough, showing resistance to the rider or lunger).

- The side-reins must help to keep the horse straight and balanced and must not be so loose and in a position that the rider's foot could accidentally become caught in them.

- Exercises will be dealt with in a subsequent section. Suffice to say that the work chosen must be appropriate to the rider's ability (as a result of assessment). The rider could be unsafe if work of too taxing a nature is attempted.

- At all times the teacher must choose work according to ongoing assessment of the rider and keep in touch with the feelings of the rider with regard to level of confidence.

- Work must always be adjusted if unforeseen circumstances dictate the need.

- The rider must safely dismount and return with the horse to the stable yard (assisted if necessary and under supervision).

When giving a lunge lesson, the Preliminary teacher must show a competence in lungeing the horse sufficiently well to also be able to teach the rider to improve. If the horse is not going well enough on the lunge then you will be limited in how effectively you can teach the rider.

2.3.4 Assessing the pupil

Assessing the pupil has been discussed to some degree in section 2.1.3, and many of the same criteria apply here. In the majority of cases the lunge lessons given by Preliminary teachers will often be directed at either beginner or novice riders. It is vital not to assume knowledge. Even if a rider has had half a dozen lessons, he may not be able to demonstrate a correct method of mounting. This is rarely because he is not trying or not interested, but more likely that with only one lesson a week, he is unable to retain the full memory of the procedure for something even as basic as mounting.

Always repeat work to find out how much retention of previous lessons there has been. The more that is retained, the more swiftly you can progress to the next stage of work. For example, a competent rider will mount quickly and efficiently because the task has become automatic, whereas the novice may take much longer just because he must recall each step and put it into action; it is not yet automatic. Remember that what seems boring and tedious to you is still exciting and challenging to the beginner rider.

- Do not assume knowledge.

- Assist the rider with mounting and adjusting stirrups and girth.

- Make the first two or three circles out on the lunge in walk to appraise the rider's basic position, thinking about the good points and then the weaker areas which will need addressing within the lesson.

- Assess the rider's confidence (body language, and verbal communication between you and him).

- Progress into trot and watch the rider in rising trot (if he can do it) and sitting trot as appropriate.

- Watch the rider particularly through the changes of pace (walk to trot and trot to walk). This is when you are most likely to see changes in the rider's balance and therefore loss of position.

- Change the rein and work similarly on the other rein.

- As a result of this initial work, plus talking to the rider about his aims and aspirations for the lesson, you should be able to decide a plan of work which will help progress the rider 'today' within this lesson.

- The novice rider will often be limited in his ideas on an aim for the lesson, so you may have to designate that in the early stages. It is important that you discuss the aim you may have chosen with the rider, so that he is quite clear on what you are trying to do, and why, within the lesson.

- As previously stated, the lesson should always be formulated as a result of the assessment.

- Within the lesson ongoing assessment is essential.

- At the end of the lesson, the same attention to detail over dismounting should be taken as was applied in the initial mounting.

- Never assume knowledge but recognise developing competence and confidence. At this stage increasingly allow the pupil to develop his own independence, while staying vigilant in your availability for support and assistance as required.

2.3.5 Improving the rider's position

Although this has been covered in section 2.1.4, I make no apology for including it again here, and reference to it will be made again in the section on the lead rein lesson. The importance of the rider developing a correct riding position cannot be over-emphasised, as it forms the foundation for the development of the rider from the earliest lessons to whatever level of competence they ultimately aspire to or achieve. The ridden horse must always be subjected to carrying the rider. The horse's way of going therefore can be greatly influenced by the way the rider sits. That influence **SHOULD** always be beneficial to the horse. Unfortunately faults in the rider's basic position can seriously inhibit the horse's correct way of going. In some cases a rider's faults can prevent him from moving with freedom, ease and regularity. No lesson, irrespective of the level of competence of the rider, is complete without reference to the basic riding position.

The following points can be specifically applied to assessing the rider's position during a lunge lesson.

- It is particularly important with a beginner or novice rider to take time at the start of the lesson to make sure that, before moving off, the rider is sitting in the centre of the saddle, as much in balance as possible.

- The beginner rider has no ability to adjust himself naturally into the centre of the saddle; often he will sit to the back of the saddle with the knee up and the lower leg therefore forward.

- The Preliminary teacher must be able to help the novice rider to sit centrally with his legs adequately stretched down, so that the stirrups are then adjusted comfortably and in a way that the correct riding position can be developed.

- The stirrups must be checked more than once to ensure that they are level and adjusted appropriately for the novice rider (not too long).

Improving the rider's position (work without stirrups and/or reins).

Once the lunge lesson commences, the size of the circle (as discussed) is essential. Too small a circle will tend to cause the rider to assume a poor position to compensate for the feeling of discomfort and loss of balance associated with riding on an over-small circle.

It is important to be aware that the continuous circle work may promote a tendency for the rider to lean inwards. As their shoulder (inside) lowers, the inside hip may collapse, and there is a likelihood that the rider's seat will slip to the outside, and therefore his balance is compromised.

It is one of the disadvantages of giving a lunge lesson that the position of the teacher (lungeing) prevents him from seeing aspects of the rider's position such as:

- Straightness in the centre of the saddle.

- Position of the rider's outside leg.

- Influence of the rider's outside leg.

It is possible, however, to make suggestions to the rider to help him focus on the areas of his position that you cannot see, so that faults do not develop and become established.

For example, you may ask the rider the following questions which would help him to concentrate on his own position:

- Where is your outside leg?

- Is your outside leg further forward or further back than your inside leg?

- Can you feel that the central seam of your jodhpurs is in line with the centre line of the saddle?

- Can you feel both your seat bones?

- Do you feel as if you have more weight on one seat bone than the other?

- Can you think of raising your inside shoulder and stretching through your waist on the inside?

- Are your shoulders parallel to, and turning with, your horse's shoulders?

Lungeing the rider enables the pupil to concentrate totally on his position and feeling the horse, as you are in control of the horse. This gives him a unique opportunity to work on his position in a way which is not possible when the horse is being ridden independently.

Work without stirrups, as discussed, will almost always help to deepen the rider's position and improve independence and feel. Work without reins is nearly always helpful in improving coordination and balance.

There is often controversy over whether a rider should be worked without reins and stirrups at the same time.

The following considerations may help you decide what is safe to do with a rider:

- If you know the horse very well (you have lunged him with a rider on many occasions before) and he is a reliable lunge horse.

- If you know the rider well (you have taught the rider several times before and know his confidence level, his physical and mental ability and his enthusiasm for achievement).

- You are teaching in a safe environment (enclosed indoor or outside school with a good surface).

- There are no apparent distractions which may disrupt your lesson.

- You have worked the rider in and the lesson is progressing positively with committed involvement of the rider.

Taking all the above factors into account, it would not be unsafe to work the rider without reins and stirrups if:

- The rider is keen to work without reins and stirrups.

- The decision to work without reins and stirrups is agreed between you and the pupil.

- The work is embarked upon after an appropriate period of warming up both horse and rider.

- The situation is ongoingly assessed, and if circumstances change then an adjustment is made to the work (e.g. give back reins or stirrups).

If the following circumstances exist:

- You have never lunged the horse before (this would be the case in an exam).

- You have never lunged the rider before (this would be the case in an exam).

- You have not worked in this school or arena before (this would be probable in an exam).

- Your knowledge of the rider (confidence, competence, physical fitness) is limited to a five or ten-minute assessment and acquaintance.

Then it would be lacking good judgment to choose to work the rider without both reins and stirrups. It is **NOT** because 'in an exam you should not lunge the rider without reins and stirrups' (as some people may try to inform you!). It **IS** because good judgment, based on the knowledge you have of the partnership, makes it inappropriate for you to choose something as taxing as this. In subsequent lessons, with greater knowledge of horse and rider, work without reins and stirrups might be both appropriate and beneficial. This point could be discussed in the theory section of the exam.

2.3.6 Work without stirrups and reins

The reference to work without stirrups and reins at the end of the preceding item leads easily into further discussion on the use of such work for riders receiving a lunge lesson.

Relaxation of the rider is an intrinsic part of developing a confident balanced, effective rider. The Preliminary teacher must learn to recognise relaxation in their pupils. Tension and anxiety has already been discussed earlier in section 2.2.2. The teacher's ongoing awareness of confidence is an essential part of a good lesson. Maintaining confidence is one of the criteria for developing and achieving progress.

Tense, nervous riders may demonstrate:

- Stiffness in their position, particularly tight shoulders and rigid arms, following through into tense, restrictive hands.

- Lower legs tight and gripping up, preventing them from sitting into the horse.

- Staccato reactions, e.g. grabbing the reins, or uncoordinated movements putting hands and legs in opposition to each other.

- Leaning forward, or less frequently leaning back, both positions putting the lower leg out of balance (either too far back or forward) and not in a position to support the upper body.

2.3.7 Exercises without stirrups, and without reins

Suppling exercises are useful to develop flexibility and coordination of the rider on the lunge.

First some work **without stirrups**:

- Encourage the rider to slip his feet out of the stirrups and allow the legs to hang down long and relaxed, by the horse's sides, for a few strides before feeling for the stirrups and taking them back. (This can be done at the halt first, and then in walk, and eventually even in trot and canter.) This exercise encourages riders to feel confident for short periods without their stirrups, and more importantly to feel that they can comfortably relocate their stirrups without effort and slip their feet in and out easily.

- During the above exercise the rider can also be encouraged to breathe deeply which will increase relaxation.

- When more serious work without stirrups is attempted it is sensible to teach the rider how to pull the stirrup buckle away from the saddle and cross the stirrups over in front of the saddle, so that the rider's legs can improve in depth and relaxation without interference from loose stirrups.

- Swinging of the lower leg from below the knee is a good flexibility exercise. Attention must always be paid to the effect that the exercise has on the rest of the body position. The position should be enhanced by the use of exercises; it must not deteriorate because of the exercise.

- Alternate leg swinging may be used.

- Drawing the knees up in front of the body so that thighs are horizontal to the ground and then stretching the legs down long and into a correct position will improve depth.

- Rotation of the ankles, both outwards and inwards, increases the depth of the seat, and relaxation of the leg and hips.

Work without reins

Work without reins should be carried out with the reins knotted. They can either be left free on the neck or the rider can have one or two fingers through the knotted end of the reins (with no contact) just to prevent the reins slipping into an unsafe position. The reins **MUST NEVER** be secured under the throat-latch of the bridle or around the neck in such a way that, in an emergency, the rider could not take up the reins for control independent of the lunger.

Arm exercises might usefully include:

- Arm circling to the rear (one arm at a time) to improve shoulder flexibility and relaxation of the upper body.

- Holding the arms out to the side, horizontal to the ground, then rotating the upper body from the waist. This exercise improves flexibility of the rider's upper body and waist and therefore relaxation and depth of seat.

- Holding the arms forward, palms down, then to the side, then above the head, can all help depth of seat.

- Placing hands onto shoulders, with upper arm horizontal to the ground and shoulders back, will help shoulder flexibility and elasticity through the neck, with neck staying back into the rider's collar.

- Any of these arm exercises can be used first in halt for the novice rider and then in walk and trot as the ability of the rider develops.

- These exercises can be developed through transitions in all paces with more experienced riders.

Constant attention to the effect of the exercises on the overall position is imperative. Any exercises must improve the position, increase depth and relaxation; they must never be used to pass the time in a lesson without recognising the effects they might be having on the rider.

It is always important to monitor the fitness of the rider throughout the lesson. If the work starts to tire the rider, then again, the benefits of the work may be lost. Adequate rest periods must always be built into any lesson. This rest time can be usefully employed to question the riders about the work, how confident they feel and whether they feel any benefit from the work. Listen to your riders, help them to develop feel, linking what they tell you to what the horse is actually doing underneath them so that they begin to feel for themselves. For example, ask them if they can feel when the horse's inside hind leg touches the ground in each walk step. If they say they can't, you then suggest that every time you say 'Now', the inside hind leg is touching the ground. Encourage them to be aware of what they feel each time you say 'now'. It may be that they feel their inside seat bone move in rhythm with the 'now'; they may feel their inside ear twitch! Whatever they repetitively feel with the 'now', that is the feel the inside hind leg gives them.

2.3.8 Dealing with problems in a lunge lesson

Dealing with problems that arise in any lesson requires tact, calmness and good judgment. Horses can be well trained, calm, obedient and equable in almost every situation but they are **NEVER** entirely predictable – **BECAUSE** they are animals. They think, feel and react occasionally with speed and unpredictability. The riding teacher must be able to deal with problems because, without a doubt, at some stage they will arise.

Problems which arise in a lunge lesson can potentially be more scary for some riders (and teachers) because of the shared control of the horse between rider and lunger. The rider is astride the horse, but the lunger is probably effecting most of the control.

The following suggestions may help you to deal with an unforeseen incident when it occurs:

- Try to reflect calmness through your voice and body language (avoid reacting with sharpness, tense voice or sudden movements).

- Assert authority through body language to regain possible lost control of the horse on the lunge.

- If the horse has speeded up and you are losing control, brace yourself in a 'sitting' position as if on a shooting stick, keeping one heel firmly into the ground so that you cannot be pulled forward by the horse. Put both hands onto the lunge rein, one behind the other, and use your voice strongly but deeply and calmly (who...oaa, stea...aady – draw your voice out long and low, but mean it!).

- Give clear and firm support and help to the rider (e.g. tell him to take hold of the front of the saddle with both hands, to try to relax and keep breathing, and to stay back with legs long).

- When the horse responds and stops, go to the horse's head and soothe him while talking to your rider to reassure him.

- Explain to the rider what happened and continue to reassure him.

- Depending on the situation, you must decide what to do next.

Sometimes, once a horse has been sensitised by an upset, whatever the cause might be, it will not be appropriate to continue the lunge lesson in the same session. It is not worth risking a repeat performance of the problem. An alternative might be to lead the horse (see lead rein lesson in the next section) or to enlist help from the yard and continue the lesson, if appropriate, with a competent leading file. The main aim must be to maintain the confidence of the pupil. Riders must learn that small problems are part of horsemanship; the experience of dealing with a problem should enhance the rider's competence and therefore his progress, and this is how he must see any problem.

The Preliminary teacher must review an incident or problem in any lesson and, if necessary with the help of a senior member of staff in the yard, make a decision as to why the incident arose. Prevention is preferable to a re-occurrence. Horses must be as reliable as possible if they are to be used for lunge lessons.

Problems reflecting the progress of the rider must be dealt with by continuous assessment and judgment of how to progress the work. In this way confidence is built and progress is steady and developing.

2.3.9 When to come off the lunge

This will depend again on ongoing assessment of competence and confidence. In general, when the beginner rider has developed the following skills, you can consider that the time is right for him to come off the lunge:

- He can lead the horse in hand, adjust stirrups and girth, and mount and dismount (with a minimum of help).

- He can adopt a correct basic riding position in halt, feeling confident (with a minimum of help) that he can choose the length of stirrup with which to ride.

- The rider can maintain a correct basic riding position in walk and trot, independent of the reins.

- He can make simple transitions from one pace to another (halt, walk and trot) both upwards and downwards while maintaining balance, independent of the reins.

- He feels confident in walk and trot without stirrups for small periods of time and through simple transitions.

The first work off the lunge would usually be a period of ten or fifteen minutes at the end of a lunge lesson. After one or two satisfactory sessions like that, the next step would be for the beginner to ride independently for the whole of a lesson but behind a more competent leading file. From this the rider should be moved into a class lesson of riders of similar competence, and then progress as a group. In the early stages of teaching fairly novice riders in a group, a more experienced leading file is always helpful. Gradually each rider within the group can develop little by little into being able to take leading file for short periods as his skill develops.

The first two or three sessions off the lunge are always quite critical. Just like a child who learns to swim with arm bands and then discards them, the first few lessons off the lunge may give the rider a feeling of being 'cut off from the lifeline of the lunge rein'. If the basic work has been securely established, this feeling will be very brief and unsustained. The first work off the lunge must be identical to the work that was carried out in the last few lunge lessons.

2.4 **The Lead Rein Lesson**

2.4.1 Suitability of the horse/pony

Lead rein lessons tend to be given to children more than to adults. Adults generally prefer to take lunge lessons or to ride in a beginner group lesson on a quiet horse, behind a competent leading file. Occasional led support from someone on the ground, as well as the instructor, can be helpful. The following information will apply to ponies and some reference will be made at the end, to any specific points which would only apply to horses used for adult lead rein lessons.

The pony used for children's lead rein lesson should have the following attributes:

- He should be cheerful when humans approach. A pony who keeps his ears forward and greets the beginner child with an enquiring gentle nuzzle of the nose is ideal.

- The pony should preferably enjoy having children around and should not show animosity towards them. (Ears back, snapping teeth or a mean attitude are not appropriate.)

- He should stand quietly for as long as might be required while the child becomes acquainted with the pony, guided by the instructor.

- He should then allow girth tightening, mounting and stirrup adjusting while continuing to stand quietly without any signs of impatience.

- Once asked to lead, he should do so willingly and with a smooth, calm manner in walk and trot on both reins, with the instructor by his side.

- When the rein is changed the pony should happily accept the instructor moving from one side to the other.

- The pony should accept the child doing some suppling exercises in halt and walk, and, if required, in trot.

- The pony should not show any adverse reaction to the child losing balance, slipping from side to side in the saddle, losing the reins or occasionally perhaps even crying while riding the pony.

- The good lead rein pony or horse should accept novice riders taking time to fumble around with the reins and stirrups because they are not yet competent and efficient.

- He should not bite at the rider when the girth is adjusted.

- Horses, especially, should be able to stand quietly beside a mounting block to enable a less mobile person to mount from a raised surface.

- They should stand still with a novice rider on board until the rider actually asks them to move or until a leader takes control of the horse.

Introducing the beginner child or adult to the horse/pony on which they will have their first riding lesson is extremely important. It is likely to have an enduring effect and impact on the whole of the rest of their riding career, however long or short that turns out to be. Almost everyone can remember their experience of riding a horse or pony for the first time ever.

Always encourage and allow your pupil to handle the horse/pony as much as possible. You must be there at all times to support and assist them, as they find the whole experience of dealing with such a large animal quite daunting. Try to remember, if you can, your first experience of having to do something with a horse/pony that you felt very nervous about, through apprehension of the unknown.

If a child is bitten, pushed about by a bossy pony or trodden on in one of his early lessons, it is very likely to have a lasting and perhaps negative effect on the child's desire to further his riding experience. It is your responsibility as the child's instructor to prevent this type of occurrence.

Horses or ponies should generally be at least five years old, so that they have been ridden for at least two years (hopefully by competent riders who help to educate them) before they are expected to cope with the inability and lack of coordination of the average beginner rider.

Horses or ponies of middle or older age will often be far more reliable and secure for the novice rider because they have had more years of accepting beginners.

Some older ponies who have been owned by a family with several brothers and sisters, and who have learnt to accept the antics that children may get up to with ponies, become ideal as lead rein ponies in a riding school in their later years.

2.4.2 Lead rein equipment

As with the lunge horse, the tack used for a lead rein lesson requires special consideration:

- It must be safely and comfortably fitted.

- It must be supple and in well-maintained condition.

- A well-fitting pony saddle of a general-purpose type is appropriate. Pony saddles are unlikely to be specific (i.e. dressage, general purpose or jumping); they should, however, fit the pony well and sit in such a way on the pony's back that the rider will be able to adopt a good basic riding position.

- If the pony is very fat and/or broad in the back (as some native ponies can be) it is important to make sure that the saddle does not slope forwards or backwards without the rider on. If it does, then it will be much more difficult, if not impossible, for the rider to adopt or maintain a correct riding position.

- The reins should not be too thick (difficult for small hands to hold or for inexperienced hands to manage).

- Similarly, over-thin reins are awkward for inexperienced hands.

- The reins should not be too long, otherwise the spare rein may dangle down the neck and there is a risk that the rider's foot may get caught in the loose loop.

- The pony should ideally be in a simple snaffle bridle with a single rein and no martingale.

- A neckstrap should be fitted.

- The pony or horse should be led from a lead rein or rope. A lunge rein is bulky with too much unnecessary rein which then needs to be managed safely.

- The lead rein or rope can either be attached to the bit on the near side of the pony (to start leading), or to a small coupling which connects both sides of the bit. This latter is a short leather connecting strap with central ring to which the lead rein is fixed.

- If the lead rein is attached to a central connector as described, there is no need to detach and reattach the lead rein on the opposite side when changing the rein; the instructor just changes side and leads from there.

- If leading directly from the bit, then of course you need to change the lead rein to the other side when you want to lead from the other side of the pony.

The horse or pony should lead easily for the person on the ground. The leader should be able to stay level with the animal's neck just in front of the shoulder. From this position you can talk easily to your pupil while maintaining good control of the horse/pony.

2.4.3 Site for lead rein lesson and safety considerations

Many of the points already discussed on safety matters apply here, but in this section the focus is on the points which are of particular relevance to the lead rein lesson and which do not necessarily apply to other lessons.

- A lead rein lesson can be safely conducted in many more situations than can a lunge lesson. This allows you more scope than a lunge lesson, regarding lesson content and format.

- A number of beginner riders can be taught in a group with one qualified or experienced instructor in the centre organising the pupils. The riders may be led by competent and experienced people who can lead horses/ponies well and safely, but are not actually instructors.

- Teaching several beginner riders separately on the lunge is far more labour-intensive than a beginner class. Lunge lessons put heavy demands on suitable horses/ponies, heavy demands on instructor availability and greater demands on viable and safe areas to use.

- A lead rein lesson can safely be conducted on a quiet bridlepath, or on a private track or road that is traffic free. This would have the added advantage of giving the rider some enjoyment and experience of riding outside an arena situation.

- A lead rein lesson can be conducted within a school where a class lesson is being given by another instructor. It would, however, be preferable that the class lesson is not a jumping lesson, unless the school is exceptionally large (20m x 60m or bigger).

Leading and supporting a child rider.

- It is not essential that a lead rein lesson is given on an artificial surface. However, the going underfoot must be good enough for the pony to move rhythmically and smoothly in walk and trot and for the leader to run comfortably alongside the pony with safe footing. A public highway would not be appropriate.

- The method of leading the pony to the area where the lesson will take place must be monitored, and where necessary support given.

- The mounting and dismounting must also be closely supervised and help given as necessary. This is covered more fully in section 2.4.5.

- If you are teaching a group of beginners or fairly novice riders then there must be space for them all to line up safely, perhaps more than once in a lesson. Riders can then listen to information while not having to think about anything else at the same time.

- If you are sharing a schooling area, it is the joint responsibility of all the instructors using the area to liaise with each other at all times to keep information flowing as to who is doing what, where. In this way riders/classes should be able to work safely in their chosen area. Naturally the larger the area concerned, the easier it is for each instructor to use their own work space.

- At all times the instructor should maintain awareness of surrounding influences which could disrupt the smoothness of the lesson they are taking.

2.4.4 Assessing the pupil

We have spoken frequently already about assessing the pupil, and the importance of ongoing assessment cannot be over-stressed. Continuous assessment of the lesson content, relevant to the responses and reactions of the pupil(s), is essential for the safe and stimulating effect of the lesson.

Assessment of the pupil starts long before the rider mounts the horse, particularly with a beginner rider, or with a rider who is new to you as the teacher, or new to the riding school. Signs are often apparent on first meeting – confidence, communication, enthusiasm and overall personality. These indicators should be absorbed by the teacher as they can help you build a picture of the pupil and assist your decision making about what work to choose later on.

The following observations give away volumes of information about a rider who says he can ride, but about whom you have scant knowledge:

- How do they approach the horse? (Cautiously, nervously, purposefully, in a brusque, 'un-horse-friendly' way.)

- How do they manage the basic handling of the horse? (Do they know how to take the reins over the head to lead in hand? Do they know where to position themselves in relation to the horse?)

- Can they lead the horse in hand? (Do they lead with purpose and authority; does the horse lead them!?)

- When they prepare to mount, how do they manage the girth, stirrups and replacing the reins over the head?

• Once mounted, what basic position do they adopt?

All these factors may be irrelevant if you are taking a beginner rider for his first lead rein lesson. They are very relevant if a rider has had a few lessons and then comes to your establishment to further his riding.

Interestingly enough, novice riders usually over-estimate their ability when explaining how much they can do, whereas more capable riders will often play down their ability and it is a pleasant surprise to find that they can ride far better than you expected.

From the first contact between you and your pupil, and then when the horse is added to the equation, you must consider all aspects of:

- Confidence.

- Developing coordination and skill.

- Competence.

- Understanding.

- Ability to cope with the physical level of activity and mental concentration.

- Surrounding influences which might affect your lesson plan and development.

It is your responsibility, throughout the lesson, to be able to justify your reasons for choosing a particular piece of work. That choice is always largely based on the criteria discussed. The choice of work must never be against your better judgment or at the rider's demand, when your 'gut' feeling is that it is not appropriate or safe.

The ultimate decision is yours, and you must always feel comfortable with it, to the best of your ability.

2.4.5 Mounting and dismounting

Learning to mount and dismount correctly is one of the most basic and important lessons the rider will ever learn. Sadly, however, it is something that many riders do incredibly badly and invariably the horse, the saddle or the rider, or all three of them, will suffer as a result. Bad mounting can create the following problems:

- A horse who is tight through the back and tense because he has had riders who:

  (a) stick their toe into his side;

  (b) heave their weight up the side of the horse, pulling him off balance and the saddle crooked;

  (c) allow their weight to land heavily and out of control onto the horse's back;

  (d) lose control of their outside leg and catch it over the cantle of the saddle or kick the horse's rump as they go over;

  (e) pull the saddle out of place to the near side, and then, once mounted, push their weight forcibly down into the off-side stirrup.

- A rider with a strained back.

- A horse who will not stand still for the rider to mount, because it is such an uncomfortable experience.

- An injured rider because the horse reacts adversely to the poor mounting technique and the rider falls off at some stage during the procedure.

As an instructor you should be passionate about good mounting and dismounting procedure, pointing out how much the horse can suffer with bad mounting and how unsafe poor mounting may prove to be.

Once riders have been taught to mount and dismount well, and then take serious responsibility for continuing good practice, they are set for life in terms of protecting their own safety and maintaining the welfare of the horse when mounting and dismounting.

Some riders (particularly small children) should be taught to mount (correctly) from a mounting block of some kind. Similarly, less agile riders, or those who are short in stature and riding a large horse, should also be encouraged to mount from a block, because it is in the best interests of the horse, the rider and the saddle. When mounting from a block, someone (preferably the rider) should always gather up the reins initially so that he is in control of the horse/pony.

A **demonstration** of a good mounting and dismounting procedure is beneficial to a beginner rider. As a Preliminary teacher you will probably be involved in teaching many beginner riders, or riders with little experience, such as those who may have 'ridden a friend's pony/horse', or been pony trekking on a holiday trail or similar. They may have had no formal instruction at all. You must be capable of explaining, step by step, exactly how to mount. This is where a demonstration is so helpful, because you can talk through the demonstration as you go. (Remember, if you are demonstrating mounting, do not waste the opportunity to demonstrate the dismount at the same time!)

If you think you are adept at describing exactly how to carry out a basic task that you find easy (because you have done it so many times before and it is automatic to you) then try this exercise with a friend (in a room, not on a wet stable floor!):

- Ask your friend to lie down flat on the floor.

- Now tell them exactly how to get up again. (Do not get on the floor and show them, or lie on the floor and think how you would get up and then describe the action – that is the easy way!)

Unless you have done this exercise before, I would almost guarantee that the only way you can explicitly tell your friend how to get up, is by getting down yourself and recalling what it is you do actually to get up again! The action is so easily automatic to you, you do not have to be able to explain it. If you are a

CORRECT MOUNTING PROCEDURE

teacher, you have to be able to explain exactly to your beginners procedures which are not automatic or even familiar to them.

Break down the mounting procedure into:

- Pick up the reins in the left hand (hold a piece of mane as well if required for stability) to prevent the horse from moving.

- Stand with your back to the horse's head (facing his tail).

- Take hold of the near-side stirrup with your right hand, turning the stirrup towards you.

- Put your left foot well into the right stirrup, keeping your toe parallel to the horse's side (not sticking into his ribs).

- Spring once or twice energetically from your right foot and push off the ground into the air.

- At the same time, using your right hand, reach over to the far side of the saddle and grasp the top of the saddle flap.

- The 'spring' should put you up in the air with your weight momentarily in your left stirrup with the left leg almost straight.

- At that point you swing your right leg high and clear of the horse's rump, and control the weight of your body so that you land softly in the saddle.

- You then take the right stirrup with your right foot and take the reins into both hands.

The dismount can be broken down into a clear procedure just as easily.

Riding is a sport, and like any other requires a varying degree of flexibility, fitness and athleticism. Horses/ponies are not just carriers for riders. Riders should learn to 'ride' their horses/ponies. They should not just be passengers, subjecting the horse to the discomfort of having to carry a heavy load who has little interest in participating in a harmonious partnership as the end product.

Mounting and dismounting for a lead rein lesson for a beginner ride should be a major part of the first few lessons. It can be made fun and interesting, to develop skill through repetition. Riders can be encouraged to develop their speed in mounting or dismounting, as they become more agile; mounting and dismounting from both sides of the horse/pony can be encouraged as a useful skill.

2.4.6 Length of lead rein lesson and choice of work

Length of lesson in relation to lungeing has already been discussed (in section 2.2.6) and similar criteria apply here. Small children (who are often given lead rein lessons) have a limited attention span. As previously mentioned, discussion may be relevant as to the age that very small children can actually benefit from formal tuition as opposed to just being led about 'on a pony' for fun.

Commercially, 30-minute private lead rein lessons for children are usually viable and realistic. If several children are taken by one instructor who gives the tuition, with each child led by a competent 'helper/leader', the session might be 30 minutes or up to 45 minutes. This might depend a little on the age of the children. Thirty minutes would be fine for children from six to ten years old. Forty-five minutes might be more appropriate for slightly older children.

The choice of work, as said on so many occasions (but in my opinion cannot be said too often), will depend on assessment and ongoing assessment. A lead rein lesson may take this format:

- Attention to mounting (and in due course dismounting) should be emphasised.

- Careful adjustment of stirrups, making sure that the rider is sitting in the centre of the saddle with legs well down under the body.

- Revision of the need to adopt a basic correct riding position should be next, with demonstration if helpful. (Demonstration can involve using another rider who may be in the school; obviously if teaching a group session, then one rider can be used to demonstrate position to the others.)

- The rider(s) will then move off in walk.

- Reiteration of basic aids for moving off will be referred to.

- Some work in walk and halt and basic left and right turns would be appropriate early work, with emphasis on position and the use of aids for basic turns and transitions.

The progression of the lesson would depend on the number of lessons the rider(s) had had, i.e. whether it was the first or tenth lead rein lesson. Fitness of the rider would also be relevant as would how often they ride. Progress when a rider rides for 30 minutes per week, will be different from a rider who can come four or five times a week.

Simple lead rein lessons should include:

- Correct mounting and dismounting.

- Ability to adopt a correct basic riding position, including how to pick up and hold the reins.

- Ability to apply simple aids to stop and start and turn left and right.

- Ability to start to work in trot.

- Introducing the concept of the trot pace, how it differs from walk in movement, speed and ways to 'ride' it (sitting or rising).

- Introducing rising trot.

- Developing rising trot and sitting trot simultaneously.

- Introducing the concept of working without stirrups.

- Exercises to develop suppleness and confidence both at halt and on the move.

- Developing all the above work as competence and confidence improves.

- The overall **aim** consists of establishing a rider who has a secure basic position, independent of the reins (i.e. never relies on the reins to maintain balance in the saddle).

- The **long-term aim** for the beginner rider should be to establish a secure, confident rider who is able to make the move into riding independently (off the lead rein) with a basic understanding of how to control the horse in simple school movements, in walk and trot in a safe enclosed area, with a more competent leading file.

- The **short-term aim** for the first lesson for a beginner might be to teach them how to mount and dismount, to adopt a correct basic riding position, and move from walk to halt and halt to walk with a clear understanding of how to achieve these, even if they need help from the leader for the first lesson.

- A **medium-term aim** for a beginner rider might be to achieve the rhythm and coordination to maintain rising trot half way around the school, with their hands off the saddle and steady.

The aims are in bold so that when sports psychology is covered in the section 2.5, these concepts will then be more easily recalled.

The choice of work in each lesson will always be directed by the confidence and state of mind of the rider and by the behaviour of the horse/pony and any outside influences (e.g. weather) which might need to be considered.

2.4.7 Teaching the correct position

Once again, I make no apology for revisiting this subject in the section on giving a lead rein lesson. The most important lesson any rider will ever learn is how to sit on a horse/pony. It forms the foundation for all future riding. Any faults which develop or become well established in the rider's early lessons will often become a nuisance later on.

Many years ago I taught a small boy to ride (in the riding school). He became a neat, competent, effective young rider. His younger sister 'learnt to ride' at home; her mother put her on a pony at an early age and the enthusiastic youngster developed the ability to 'stay on' in walk, trot and canter and over a jump. This girl always had unsteady hands and a loose position with a tendency to 'swing around' on the horse's back. I worked hard on her in her teenage years, to help her to develop the security in her seat which would stabilise her hands and help her to ride with more balance and effect. Established faults are always harder to eradicate than building the correct foundation in the first place.

Once the beginner rider has been introduced to the pony/horse he is to ride and

A good position, showing correct shoulder-hip-heel alignment.

As rider's leg goes forward, upper body goes back behind movement and out of balance.

The rider's body tips forwards, the leg slips too far back and the rider is again out of balance.

has learnt how to lead him in hand, how to check the girth and pull down the stirrups ready for mounting, then a correct mounting procedure would be followed. This procedure would be part of every lead rein lesson, so gradually the rider should develop greater ability to manage these early tasks himself with the minimum of help from you.

In every situation, but particularly with a new pupil, this early format must be closely monitored, with help and advice offered if there are gaps in the rider's knowledge.

Once the rider is mounted:

- If necessary, the rider should be helped to find the centre of the saddle in which to sit.

- Encourage the seat to come forward if necessary (usually it is pushed back with the knee up and in front of the rider).

- Encourage the knees to stretch down and suggest to the rider that he is trying to aim for a position where his shoulder will be above his hip, and his hip above his heel, thereby having an imaginary straight line from ear, through hip, to heel, to give balance to the upper body over the lower leg.

It can be helpful to show your rider, from the ground, what happens when you lean forward (your leg goes back and you tip forward out of balance); conversely, what happens when you lean back and your leg goes forward (again you fall back out of balance, because your leg no longer supports your upper body).

Once you start moving the rider around within the lesson, monitoring of the position is essential. If you are teaching from the middle (with each beginner being led by a competent leader) it is relatively easy to watch each rider's position and make helpful corrections to assist him in maintaining a good position. If you are actually leading the pony/horse and giving the instruction at the same time, this is not so easy. You are close to the pony and a little in front of your pupil, so clear observation from the side view is not so easy.

Often a reminder to the rider to maintain his position is as helpful as correcting it once a fault arises.

It would be sensible to encourage the rider to check his position:

- Before he makes a turn or change of direction.

- Before he makes a change of pace (upwards or downwards transition).

- At regular intervals whenever they think of it.

Your teaching should encourage the riders to think of their position often.

Often Preliminary teachers think of position work as 'boring' and 'repetitive'. Boring it should never be, repetitive it is; but the way you teach it must be stimulating and challenging. You need to encourage your riders to want to sit as well as they possibly can because they realise its importance and relevance to their future riding.

2.4.8 Work without stirrups/reins

Re-read the information on this subject in section 2.3.6 and 2.3.7. Much of the text is similar. I would, however, emphasise the importance of this work and in this section try to cover information which could be regarded as specific to a lead rein lesson.

While the pony/horse is being led the animal should be under the total control of the leader. With this in mind there should be minimal risk of the rider losing balance to the point of falling off. The leader is close enough and should be sufficiently aware, to take hold of the rider's nearside leg (if leading from the left side) to help stabilise him and prevent him from slipping out of balance. This may be necessary with a very small child, but should rarely be necessary in other cases unless:

- An unforeseen situation causes the pony/horse to react and move suddenly or unexpectedly.

- The work chosen causes the rider to slip or lose balance unexpectedly.

It can be helpful for the child on the lead rein to slip his feet out of his stirrups, stretch his legs long and feel for his stirrups again. This encourages the rider to feel for his stirrups rather than look down for them, or, worse still, take hold of the stirrup leather and pull the iron up to meet the foot.

Working without stirrups for short periods should, for the most part, be an integral part of any lead rein lesson. The riders should be shown initially how to cross their stirrups over in front of the saddle. They should understand why:

- The buckle should be pulled away from the stirrup bar before the leather is folded over. (So that the leather lies flat.)

- The right stirrup should be crossed first and the left stirrup second. (So that if re-mounting is required while the stirrups are crossed, the left one can be pulled down and is not lying under the other one.)

- The stirrups should be on the pony's neck in front of the saddle, not on the saddle itself. (If on the saddle, the stirrups would be in the way of the rider.)

As already mentioned, the horse/pony is under the total control of the leader. Work without stirrups could therefore be carried out with:

- The rider's hands resting on the pommel of the saddle (reins knotted and loose on the neck, or just the buckle end of the knotted reins held in one of the rider's hands.)

- One hand on the saddle, one hand either in rein position (not holding the reins) or as described holding the buckle end.

Beginner riders would start by having short periods of work without stirrups in walk, making transitions from halt to walk and walk to halt. As their confidence and ability developed, then some periods in trot could be included. The rider should be encouraged to 'sit' to the trot finding relaxation in his back, legs stretching long, to enable him to balance in the centre of the saddle.

As always, the teacher should observe and assess the effect of the work on the rider's progress and confidence.

Similarly, working without reins can be carried out with the same considerations:

- The rider should be encouraged to feel confident about resting knotted reins on the neck and holding one or both hands in the 'rein position'.

- Working without reins would involve similar work to that described for work without stirrups.

The aim is to develop a rider who feels confident in his own balance and coordination in the saddle and never feels a need to rely on the reins to keep himself in position.

It is acceptable to work without reins and stirrups in a lead rein lesson as long as:

- You know the horse/pony well and have given many lead rein lessons with him before.

- You know the rider, having taught them on some previous occasions.

- The environment appears to be trouble-free (no adverse weather or nearby noisy distractions).

- The area being used is enclosed and on a consistent surface.

- You have the confidence and understanding of the rider, who is keen to progress.

Many of these factors would not exist in an examination situation so it would be a wise judgment to choose something less challenging. It does not mean that working without reins and stirrups at the same time is unsafe.

2.4.9 Lead rein exercises

The use of exercises has been discussed with reference to the lunge lesson and many exercises used for lunge lessons can also benefit the rider on the lead rein. Here we will try to cover some exercises which are appropriate for riders being led or standing still while the pony/horse is held.

Exercises which would be appropriate for riders while being led could include:

- Arm circling (one at a time and both together) backwards to improve shoulder position and overall upper body suppleness.

- Shoulder shrugging (backwards) to improve shoulder and neck suppleness.

Without stirrups

- Lower leg swinging from the knee down (alternate legs and both legs at the same time).

- With legs and arms it is more taxing to ask the rider to circle one arm backwards while the other arm circles forward (tests coordination); similarly this can be done with the legs (slightly easier).

- Drawing both knees up in front and then stretching both legs down long.

- Ankle circling, toes outwards and toes inwards. (Supples the lower leg.)

The following exercises can be carried out at the halt, with each pony/horse being held individually by one leader. Riders can take their feet out of the stirrups, but the stirrups can be left hanging down the saddle. The reins should be knotted and resting on the neck.

- With hands on hips, the rider leans back until his shoulders and head are resting on the pony's back. He then sits up gradually. (Stretches and strengthens stomach muscles, improves confidence and suppleness of upper body.)

- The rider sits on sideways, then sits facing backwards, then sits on facing the other side and then sits forwards again. This exercise, sometimes known as 'round the world' (for children), improves balance, confidence and coordination. It can ultimately be done with hands on hips where balance is well tested also. At no time should the rider kick the pony with a leg as he manoeuvres himself around. With children, this exercise can usefully be turned into a race to see which child can complete the round the quickest – as long as with speed they do not compromise quality of movement and end up being rough on the pony. This must be strictly controlled by the teacher.

- With left hand on hip and right hand above head, the rider leans down to touch right toe. The rider must stretch the leg long, not bring the leg up to meet the hand.

- Same exercise, but right hand leaning over to touch left toe. This requires more stretch and suppleness. The rider's outside leg must not lose position as the rider leans over to touch the opposite toe.

■ These exercises can be repeated with left arm to left toe and left arm to right toe.

These exercises are only beneficial at a standstill. On the move they could be detrimental to good position because they are requiring the rider to lean forward and the pony's movement would further push them out of balance.

There are one or two other exercises, requiring greater confidence and coordination, which can be carried out on a horse/pony at the halt. These are not, however, the remit of a beginner or novice rider having a lead rein lesson.

2.4.10 When to come off the lead rein

When a beginner takes lead rein lessons and asks how many lessons he may need on the lead rein before riding independently, the answer cannot be finite. It will depend on:

■ His confidence.

■ How often he rides (riders riding several times a week will progress more quickly than a once-a-week rider).

■ The instructor – to a degree the level of instructor may influence progress. The more experienced instructor should be able to progress a rider a little more quickly than a young instructor of less experience.

■ The rider's natural flair to take instruction in riding. (Some people take to riding like a 'duck to water', others are far more cautious.)

■ His commitment and effort.

As the rider progresses, he should feel more balanced and in control of the horse/pony himself. The leader should gradually be handing over more and more responsibility to the rider for the control of the horse/pony.

Initially the rider will make turns and changes of direction and pace with the support of the leader. Eventually he should be fully influencing the horse/pony, with only the accompaniment of the leader. When this stage is reached then the pupil should have five or ten minutes at the end of a lesson 'off the lead rein' to begin to practise his new-found ability. This period off the lead rein will gradually extend, over perhaps three or four lessons, until the whole session could be independent. At this stage the rider would either join a small class of riders of a similar standard with one competent leading file to assist, or be integrated into a group where one rider with a little more experience off the lunge or lead rein is capable of being leading file. (See also section 2.3.9.)

2.5 Sports Psychology

THIS SECTION DISCUSSES some of the areas of sports psychology and child protection that are now intrinsic in any sports coaching. Many of the concepts of sports psychology are ideas that have been used for generations by teachers of many subjects, both academic and sporting. In recent years we have identified certain aspects of sports psychology that can be utilised to make major improvements in sporting performance at any level, from beginner to world class competitor, not only by working to improve a rider's technical skill, but also by addressing his psychological approach. In the simplest form the Preliminary teacher must begin to take on these concepts as a basis for their future teaching and helping pupils at all levels. They must be aware of their responsibilities with regard to teaching children a sport.

2.5.1 Lesson planning

There has already been some reference to lesson planning, but the subject deserves further consideration here.

Some lesson planning and preparation means that the teacher has given some thought and consideration to a lesson before embarking on working with an individual or group. Prior knowledge of whom you are to teach obviously enables you to consider a relevant plan. I have also referred frequently and throughout this text to the need to assess and continue to assess as a basis for choosing work. If we consider the class lesson you will be required to teach in the Preliminary Teaching Test, we can discuss the planning before and within this session.

The class lesson will be to a group of three or four riders of basic riding ability, capable of walk, trot and canter and negotiating basic jump work such as ground poles and small fences up to about 2ft 6in. (75cm).

The other prior knowledge you have is that the class lesson will take place in an indoor school with a minimum area of 20m x 40m.

This information means that you could plan:

- Where you will line up the ride to introduce yourself and your lesson subject. (Line up the ride within close proximity to your examiner, so that he can hear you.)

- How your ride will move off. (Probably in closed order to allow you to assess basic position and overall control.)

- You could have some ideas about the basic school movements you might use in the initial assessment, e.g. how you might change the rein.

- Whether you see walk, trot and canter in the early part of the lesson would probably depend on your initial and ongoing assessment.

- You can make your plan knowing how long you will have to teach (about 35 minutes). You must be able to monitor your own time and keep the lesson moving along.

- You can plan for any lesson to have an introduction, a main content of teaching and a period of conclusion and summing up to finish the lesson. Avoid starting anything new in the last period of any lesson (since doing so could produce problems you do not have time to deal with).

Your more specific lesson plan would depend on:

- The lesson subject you were given at the briefing at the start of your exam.

- All the lesson subjects will start with 'Assess your rider's ability...' (The full list is given in the appendix of this book.)

- All the lesson subjects are aimed at encouraging you to:

  (a) Teach what you see in front of you;

  (b) Teach to improve basic principles of good horsemanship, e.g. position, balance, feel, coordination, correct aid application.

Your lesson plan must reflect your awareness of your riders' ability.

Let's assume your lesson subject is to 'assess your riders' ability over a single fence, and then using several fences work to improve their position and feel', and in your initial assessment you find that one or more riders is unbalanced, nervous and not in control of their horse. In this case you must improve their balance, confidence and therefore control, and only move on to the jumping if you have the riders in a situation to start the jumping safely. Do not aim just to 'teach the brief'. If the assessment reveals that the subject would be difficult to teach until the other problems have been addressed then, in the interests of safety, welfare of riders and horses and good teaching practice, you must improve what you see.

2.5.2 Motivation

What is 'motivation'? Another word for motivation is 'incentive'.

- What gives someone the incentive to want to learn to ride?

- What gives someone the motivation to want to win a show-jumping class?

- What gives you the incentive to want to take and pass your Preliminary Teaching Test?

You can probably give the answer to the last question. (I certainly hope so!)

Motivation is what 'drives' someone to want to achieve something.

Teachers who work in a secondary school may be dealing with a number of children who have no 'incentive' to be there at all. For riding teachers that is not so common. Most people who come to learn to ride do have a motivation to do it. That motivation may be:

- Their friend rides so they want to.

- They have a sister or brother who rides.

- They always wanted to since seeing show jumping on television.

- They always wanted to because they love horses.

If a rider is self-motivated then your job as a Preliminary teacher is to maintain that motivation.

Let us consider what can enhance motivation:

- Enjoyment of the first lesson, and a desire to enjoy another one.

- Liking the horse they ride.

- Liking the instructor.

- Having fun within a lesson with other like-minded people.

- Finding that they can achieve (managed rising trot, first canter, first jump, etc.).

So what could lower motivation?

- Not enjoying the lesson. (Bitten by the horse when they led it out unsupervised, trodden on when they tried to mount, run away with on the first lesson!)

- Not liking the horse. (See above points – need I say more?)

- Not liking the instructor. (Feeling abandoned, belittled, inadequate because of the manner of the teacher.)

- Feeling frightened and incapable in a lesson.

- Feeling completely out of control of the horse and the whole situation.

From this brief resume, you should see that 'motivation' can never be defined as being a constant. Motivation is variable and fragile and can be directly affected by you as the teacher. What you do in a lesson, how you treat your pupils and how you manage their mental state can benefit or adversely affect the outcome of any lesson.

2.5.3 Goal setting

If you look back to section 2.4.6 you will see highlighted the short-term, medium-term and long-term goal or aim. Here we will look more closely at the concept of goal setting. We have discussed assessment with regard to planning. Goal setting is about being able to set small aims or targets for any rider under any situation. These aims/goals or targets must be:

- Clearly identifiable. (For example, the rider wants to learn to canter.)

- Measurable.

- Realistic.

- Achievable.

If the goals do not fulfil the above criteria then the presence of them may prove to be demotivating to the rider, and the goal, rather than enhancing motivation and progress, actually does the opposite. For example, if a person who had never ridden before, was in their mid-fifties and had never been involved in any active sport before, came to you having watched Badminton Horse Trials on the television, saying she wanted you to teach her to ride well enough to tackle Badminton next year(!), the goal would be totally unrealistic and almost certainly unachievable. In maintaining that as the aim, the motivation would almost certainly suffer as the achievement became more and more unlikely. Your job as the teacher would be to adjust the goal to something more realistic. For your keen beginner put in three goals:

- A short-term goal: Have your first riding lesson (by the end of the month).

- A medium-term goal: Be riding independently (off the lead rein or lunge line) in walk and trot (in six months).

- A long-term goal: Be able to walk, trot and canter confidently (in twelve months), and then you will take your pupil to spectate at Badminton rather than just see it on television.

Setting goals is in itself motivating as long as the goals are constantly reviewed and adjusted. By always setting achievable goals, which then are achieved, continued motivation is assured.

2.5.4 Dealing with success and failure

The areas of sports psychology which are highlighted in this section are all inherently linked.

How a person deals with success and failure in any avenue of his life can constructively or adversely affect other areas of his existence. The riding teacher, as any other teacher, has a responsibility to his pupils to understand the process of success and failure and to give some thought as to how it might affect a lesson.

As a Preliminary teacher taking a class lesson you may use an exercise which half the group manage well and one or two cannot achieve. How do you deal with this?

A worse scenario might be where one rider falls off during a class lesson and considers the fall to be his own fault. He becomes increasingly upset that he is 'useless and not as good as the rest of the class'. How you deal with these situations can rebuild a rider's self-esteem and confidence, or help to destroy it.

When your pupils feel successful (manage rising trot, achieve their first canter) their success builds confidence and self-esteem – it is therefore motivating. Similarly if a rider begins to feel a failure, self-esteem drops, confidence wanes and a downward spiral begins, leading to a negative, nervous rider, full of self-doubt.

Give some thought to success and failure:

- How does success make you feel?

- How does failure make you feel?

- As a teacher, how should you support someone who feels they are failing or not very good at something?

- If a pupil is achieving well, is there a point at which success can become a problem to further development?

- How do you recognise a pupil who is getting over-confident through success? Should you do anything about it?

2.5.5 Dealing with stress and anxiety

Dealing with stress and anxiety is a part of everyday life – whether it is the stress of preparing for your Preliminary Teaching Test or the anxiety of waiting for the results. Stress and anxiety are part of our existence.

How one identifies stress or anxiety, and how one copes with these issues, are part of your responsibility as a teacher. With this consideration, we will give some thought as to how you deal with stress and anxiety as a Preliminary teacher. Interestingly, what is stressful to one person is not necessarily the same for others. What causes anxiety to you may not cause anxiety to your friend.

Stress can be defined as 'physical or mental pressure'.

Anxiety can be defined as 'state of apprehension or doubt'.

Recognising these states of mind in your riders is essential if you are to be a sympathetic and helpful teacher. Work that you choose to do within your lesson plan may put some riders into a stressful state or make them anxious. Within the assessment and the ongoing programme of work you must be able to:

- Monitor your riders constantly and communicate with them through discussion so that you are always aware of their feelings about the work.

- Adjust the lesson plan at any time so that the rider's mental state is accommodated.

Stress can be either positive or negative depending on how it is managed. Stress raises the body's awareness and reaction. Due to the production of the hormone adrenaline within the system, the body's flight-and-fight mechanism is heightened. This can improve the rider's commitment and effort, and with a competitive rider can give them the 'edge' to win. Conversely, if the stress becomes too great, then the individual cannot cope with the 'pressure', and a sharp deterioration in performance is the result.

The teacher's job is to monitor carefully the progress of work so that:

- Motivation is high.

- Self-esteem is generated.

- Success and achievement is further motivating.

- While the work is challenging it maintains a controllable stress level which produces the maximum response of the rider without 'going over the top' by putting the person under stress that they cannot deal with.

Anxiety can also be challenging and constructive, but the teacher has the ultimate control of knowing how far an uninitiated rider can be pushed to attempt to achieve a little more. This is a critical point, and communication with the pupil is essential and should be ongoing. The teacher will understand the implications of the work they are choosing.

For example, you, as a Preliminary teacher, will understand when the beginner rider has sufficient ability to learn to canter. Your pupil does not have that knowledge and therefore must rely on your judgment. When you say he should be trying canter, if he trusts you and has confidence in you, then he should be positive about wanting to try. At this point he may still feel anxious. His anxiety stems from:

- Attempting something as yet untried and unknown.

- Apprehension about whether he will manage.

- Doubt as to whether he is in fact good enough, even though you say he is.

You must never try to push a rider beyond the point where he can cope. If you do, then anxiety may develop into fear, and this is a very negative emotion which has a severely limiting effect on performance.

Teaching is an ongoing balancing act, especially where group lessons are concerned. The ability to develop each rider's skill within his own individual parameters of confidence, anxiety and stress is indeed a talent which you will develop throughout your teaching career.

Some riders enjoy the 'buzz' that an injection of stress gives them; others are the opposite, and are content never to be pushed beyond the zone in which they feel one hundred per cent comfortable. The latter have ultimately to recog-

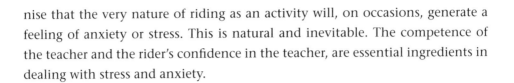

nise that the very nature of riding as an activity will, on occasions, generate a feeling of anxiety or stress. This is natural and inevitable. The competence of the teacher and the rider's confidence in the teacher, are essential ingredients in dealing with stress and anxiety.

2.5.6 The difference between teaching children and adults

Teaching is about transferring knowledge or skill from one person to another. As a Preliminary teacher you will be involved with teaching children and adults. Riders of mixed ages can enjoy class lessons together (parents may wish to ride with their children, for example), and certainly when hacking and riding out, you will probably be responsible for mixed groups. There are some considerations and differences to be taken into account in the way that you might teach children as opposed to adults.

Considerations when teaching children:

- Depending on their age, children have a much smaller concentration span than adults. You may need to split up the periods of serious tuition with plenty of less intense riding. (Include games, exercises and watching each other to maintain enthusiasm.)

- Children may physically be too small to control the pony in some work.

- Children require only the most basic information about how to do something. They cannot process series of information.

- Children may be very influenced by seeing someone else do something (good outcome or not).

- Children will often 'follow' someone else's example, even though they may not be capable of achieving what the other person has.

- Children have very little awareness of 'what could go wrong' until it actually happens.

- Children very rarely have reason not to trust you and they believe in you implicitly – until they have a good reason not to. On this basis try never to induce a situa-

Supporting a child rider from the ground, e.g. for the first canter.

tion where a child rider has reason to doubt your judgment.

Considerations when teaching adults:

■ Adults often have a very good theoretical knowledge of what they want to do (they have often read many books on the subject) but their physical ability is well behind their mental appreciation of the subject.

■ Intelligent adults who are successful in their own work environment are often very frustrated when they take up riding and the progress is, in their opinion, very slow.

■ Adults have a great capacity for taking in as much technical information as is available; often they have a very analytical approach to their faults and how to remedy them.

■ Adults are often very aware of all that could go wrong (e.g. how far it is to the ground, how quickly the horse appears to be going out of control).

- Adults are often very aware of what they consider their own limitations to be and will not necessarily be tempted to try something that they feel is beyond their ability, just because they see someone else doing it.

- Adults may have definite physical limitations in flexibility and mobility.

- Adults tend to believe more in their own judgment than in yours when it comes to things they think they can or cannot do. On this basis, if in doubt, don't pressurise someone to attempt something.

2.5.7 Child protection in equestrian sport

Being in charge of children as their teacher, raises issues whereby you must safeguard the children in your care and your own position with the children. Similarly you must ensure that they are always safe and feel comfortable with you in a position of authority over them.

Once you have achieved your PTT, before you can become a member of the BHS Register of Instructors (see Appendix 7), among other requirements it will be necessary for you to attend a short half-day course to train you in issues relevant to child protection in sport. The highest priority must be placed on the safety and enjoyment of children involved in riding. A duty of care means that you, as an instructor (with the riding school or senior instructor under whom you work), must ensure that all reasonable steps are taken to safeguard the safety of any individual involved in any activity for which you, the instructor, or the school is responsible.

With this in mind as a Preliminary teacher you should be able to discuss the following subjects as they relate to you as a teacher in charge of children:

- What is a duty of care with regard to child protection?

- What age is classified as a 'child'?

- Discuss examples of good practice when teaching children.

- What sorts of things might be considered poor practice?

- What sorts of problem can there be with over-anxious parents watching their child's lessons?

- Understand the difference between verbal, physical or mental abuse.

- Know what to do if you feel a child in your care is suffering abuse under any circumstances.

- Know what to do if you have concerns about the welfare of any child you are teaching.

Being aware of your responsibilities as a teacher in charge of children will also safeguard your own position in the event that you are accused of bad practice in any circumstances. Young male instructors, in particular, should be aware that adolescents can find members of the opposite sex very attractive and may fantasise about the way they feel about those in authority over them. School teachers, and sports coaches (in this case of equestrian sport), must take sensible measures to make sure they are never in a compromising situation with any pupil without realistic support nearby. Situations can easily be misinterpreted and the young instructor should always have the benefit of someone to corroborate the exact circumstances.

2.6 Lecturette and Written Paper

DURING ONE OF THE THEORY/DISCUSSION sessions of the Preliminary Teaching Test you will be asked to give a short talk or lecturette of about 5 minutes duration. This would be as if to Stage 1 trainees or Pony Club 'C' Test youngsters. You will be given the title of your lecture at the briefing at the beginning of your exam day. The subject will be a simple stable management topic, such as:

- The advantages and disadvantages of using a New Zealand rug.

- Reasons for grooming.

- Checking a saddle for safety.

- Catching horses/ponies up for work.

The examiner is looking for the way you have thought out the subject, and done some simple preparation to enable you to deliver a short, concise but clear explanation of your subject. You must show confidence as you stand up and speak clearly to your audience (your co-candidates) and have the content of your lecture well organised.

2.6.1 Lecturette structure

Any lecture, whatever its length, should have a clear structure. That structure would usually incorporate:

- An introduction – of yourself, if necessary, and certainly of your subject.

- The main body of the talk – this would cover the major content of the subject.

- A conclusion – this would include a brief summing up of the main points of your talk and be neatly concluded by a closing statement. For example (on the subject 'checking a saddle for safety'): 'I have covered the main aspects of how to check a saddle for safety and would remind you that safety is of paramount importance in the interests of the welfare of both horse and rider. Are there any questions?... Thank you.')

Giving a very short lecture can be quite difficult, especially if you have a large amount of information on the subject. You must be able to prioritise the most important points to be put across. It is easy to try to include too much, and then be tempted to hurry, rushing to fit in all that you have thought of or written down in notes. That is why some preparation is essential. It should allow you to decide which are the most important facts to include.

The facts must be correct; if in doubt, do not use information of which you cannot be sure.

If it helps you to jot down some brief notes to help you in delivering the talk, then jot down a few points on a small notepad or postcard. These notes can then be used discreetly during your delivery, especially if you are worried that you may 'get tongue-tied' or run out of things to say.

You must never resort to reading your notes as if reading a text to your audience.

If you are asked to bring your lecture to a close before you have completed, then one of three things usually happens.

- The lecturer increases the speed of his delivery in an effort to cover all the information still left to discuss, even though there will be an over-run of time or time will run out completely.

- The lecturer stops in mid-sentence, and leaves the subject and his audience verbally abandoned with no smooth conclusion.

- The lecturer tails off in his delivery and everyone is left somewhat in a state of limbo as they wait for the lecturer to decide the next move.

If you are asked to stop then the procedure should be as follows:

- Finish the sentence you were making, if applicable.

- State that unfortunately you have been asked to finish and so you are unable to complete the full content of the subject as you had wished. You hope to be able to finish the subject on another occasion … Are there any questions?

- Never be pressurised into trying to complete the subject matter, unless you are allowed more time.

A well-structured, well-delivered informative lecture is the main aim of this section of the exam.

2.6.2 Lecturette content

The content of your lecturette will depend very greatly on the subject, of course. It is of utmost importance, however, that the information you give is:

- Correct factually.

- Delivered in an organised way.

- Concise and to the point.

- Not repetitive.

Introducing yourself is important and gives you the opportunity to 'break the ice' with your audience. It would not be necessary to ask or learn your audience's names, but it is helpful to state the subject of your talk and if you want to, write the title on a blackboard or white board.

The main body of the subject should be enough to fill about four of your five minutes. It may be split up into several headings, if this is appropriate to your subject. Splitting up the content of your talk helps to maintain interest from your audience.

For example, if your lecture subject was 'Use of a New Zealand rug' you might split up the main content as follows:

- Basic description – 'What is a New Zealand rug?'

- When is it used and why?

- What are the advantages of a NZ rug?

- What are the disadvantages of a NZ rug?

- How do you look after the rug?

Remember, there is no set format for giving a short talk. You must show some ability to break down basic stable management subjects into information that a less knowledgeable audience can clearly follow and understand.

Take a basic stable management book to the exam if you want to and use it briefly when preparing your lecture. It must be your work and your preparation. Using your trainer as a prompter is never satisfactory because the lecturette must be **YOURS**, not a concoction of your work with a large contribution from your trainer.

2.6.3 Lecturette delivery

Standing up in front of any audience, particularly one containing examiners, will probably be a very nerve-racking experience. Many candidates feel this is the most difficult section because of the close proximity of the examiner. Whereas in the class lesson you quickly become absorbed in the task of working with your pupils, in the lecture delivery it is very easy to 'feel the examiner's eyes on you'. To overcome this nervousness you must practise giving short talks and lectures as often as you possibly can before your exam. Even if you give the information to an imaginary audience, your family, the dog or a mirror, you must **PRACTICE**, because through practice you will gradually become more competent and therefore at ease.

There are several points which may help you to improve your delivery. We have already covered structure and content and these are important because they will then allow the information that you are delivering to come across in an organised and clear way.

Consider the following to improve delivery:

- You must try to speak clearly and not too fast. Nerves often cause the voice to become higher and quicker – this is usually because you forget to breathe well.

- Breathe slowly and deeply and practise pausing at the end of each sentence. This will allow your words to have impact on the audience and will also encourage you to breathe before you start the next sentence.

- Teach yourself to speak, pause, breathe and speak again.

- Try to enunciate each word carefully. Your words will carry across a room with more clarity if you maintain the strength of your voice through to the end of the word. Do not allow your voice to tail off at the end of each word or at the end of a sentence because then your words will lose impact.

- If your talk is divided in any way – say, under a main heading and then perhaps with one or two sub headings – make sure that your delivery clearly indicates those divisions. A slightly longer pause is needed to define these.

- Try to look at your audience. Even if you do not feel brave enough to make full eye contact with anyone, learn to look generally at your listeners. Looking down does not create a feeling of involvement or authority, both of which you should want to create.

- Ideally your eyes should slowly rove over the audience, resting your gaze briefly on one specific person from time to time – not to a point where they feel uncomfortable, but just so that they feel you are speaking 'to them specifically'.

- Try to create some variation in your voice, which will maintain interest for those listening. If everything you say is delivered in a monotone, no matter how interesting the subject, it will sound boring.

- Standing up to deliver your talk will create a better impression of professionalism and authority. Whilst it is quite acceptable to sit down if you really prefer, sitting tends to often convey a more casual approach and may lack a degree of impact.

- When standing up try to adopt a confident but relaxed pose.

- Avoid leaning against something. This looks casual and may end up as a 'slouch'.

- Avoid having your hands in your pockets (again, casual) or arms folded across chest (sends out negative body language signals).

- Try to allow your arms and hands to be relaxed by your side or behind your back. Learn to adopt a comfortable pose that is easy for you. Mannerisms that are repetitive (e.g. tapping fingers on the table, or fiddling with a pen) may be very irritating and distracting for an audience.

- If the examiner asks you to bring your talk to a close and you still have much that you want to say:

DO NOT

- Increase the speed of your delivery, turning your voice into a monotone of words that run into each other in your effort to say everything in the limited time left.

- Stop instantly, leaving everyone feeling as if they have been cut off abruptly from the fluent supply of information.

DO

- Finish the sentence or part of the subject you were currently covering and tell your audience that there was a little more you wished to say but unfortunately you have been asked to stop.

- Ask the audience if they have any questions on what you have said and suggest that on another occasion you would like to say more on the subject.

- Finish what you were saying as concisely and efficiently as you can without breaking off abruptly.

- Imagine a genuine situation where you were called away due to an unforeseen circumstance: you would never just abruptly stop talking and abandon your audience without explaining why you had to leave.

You will give your lecturette at some time during one of the theory sessions in the exam. You may be first to go, or you may watch and listen to other candidates in your group as they give their lectures before you. Whichever the situation, be prepared to go first, last or in the middle. Try to stay calm while waiting for your turn. Concentrate on breathing deeply and regularly as this will keep your body well supplied with oxygen, which helps keep your brain sharper and your nerves at bay.

If you are not first to go, then try not to waste the time while you are waiting. In addition to breathing deeply, visualise where you will stand in relation to the audience and the blackboard or whiteboard. In five minutes it is not really practical to use the board, other than for writing up your subject as a focus and reminder.

ONLY use the black/white board if you can write:

■ Clearly, and big enough to be legible.

■ Straight.

■ Spell **CORRECTLY.**

If in doubt, don't use the board.

Your lecturette is there to show that you have the ability to put together a clear, well-structured talk on a simple stable management subject and then can deliver the correct information in a pleasant and audible voice.

2.6.4 Written paper

At some stage during the Preliminary Teaching Test examination you will be required to write a short written paper. This part of the test will last about 30 minutes and will involve you writing on a very practical subject that might be your responsibility in employment as a Preliminary teacher.

The type of subject that might be covered will be:

■ Filling in an accident report form.

■ Writing up a livery form for a newly arrived horse coming into the yard to board.

■ Writing out a specimen feeding chart for a 'new horse' in the yard.

• Writing out a risk assessment, e.g. for a class jumping lesson.

While you will not actually be examined on:

(a) your writing clarity or legibility;

(b) your spelling;

(c) your presentation of the information;

(d) your organisation of the facts;

it is nevertheless important that you write as clearly as you can and that you present the work in as neat a fashion as you can. This is because:

- In the case of something like an accident report form, your work may be used subsequently in any legal proceedings that might result from questioning the circumstances of the incident.

- It conveys a much more professional image of the establishment.

- You should take pride in any work that you produce.

- Someone may have to read your work at a later stage and be able to understand it. (In the first instance, the examiner can only mark work that he can read and understand.)

Practise producing neat and well-planned written work.

Study a BHS accident report form (see appendix) and make sure that if you have never had to fill one in before or seen one being completed, that you ask your trainer or more senior instructor to show you exactly what should be included. In the exam you will be given an 'imaginary scenario' and you will have to complete the form using the details given to you, imagining that you were teaching the lesson or in charge of the hack when the accident occurred.

Similarly, if you had to run through the details that are recorded in 'your yard' when a new horse comes in at livery, this would probably include:

- Name of horse and name of owner.

- Address and telephone number of owner (home number and work or mobile, if necessary).

- Details of horse (size, breeding, age, sex).

- When the horse was last shod / wormed / received inoculation boosters.

- What the horse has come for (schooling, while owner on holiday, etc.).

- What type of livery the horse will be on (part, full, working).

- Details of the owner's own vet (if to be used).

- What equipment the horse has come with. (List separately.)

- Special diet or supplementary feeding the horse is currently on.

- Any special additional points (e.g. horse chews his rugs, doesn't eat sugar beet, etc.).

In planning a feed regime for a specific horse, again you would be given some information about the horse, from which you should be able to make a plan. The type of information you would need to be able to plan a feedchart would include:

- Horse's height and type (e.g. Thoroughbred or cob)

- Age and temperament.

- Type of work he is doing.

- Whether the horse spends any time turned out at grass each day.

In working out a risk assessment your priorities would be:

- To make a thorough breakdown of the task or session (e.g. clipping a horse, or giving a class jumping lesson).

- By itemising each part of the task you can then consider where there are any areas of risk.

- By highlighting the possible areas of risk you can then put in place a procedure to minimise that risk. For example, you identify that when taking a class of four children out to the school for a jumping lesson, if they line up in a haphazard way then someone may get kicked. By implementing a policy of always lining up in a straight line for mounting then this risk is identified and minimised.

The written paper is there to demonstrate that as a Preliminary teacher you can maintain basic records which are relevant to a commercial establishment dealing with the general public. You must be capable of taking telephone messages and writing down relevant notes for your senior instructor or yard manager.

Records of veterinary or medical importance, whilst not being your primary responsibility, may become your remit, if only because in an emergency (e.g. a horse ill with colic, or a rider injured in an accident) the more senior member of staff may be immediately involved with the crisis.

A competent Preliminary teacher will be able to take verbal messages and where necessary write down relevant information to be handed on to a more senior member of staff as and when appropriate.

Appendices

STAGE 3
GROOM'S CERTIFICATE

THE BRITISH HORSE SOCIETY
Registered Charity No. 210504

....

was examined in Horse Knowledge and Care, and attained the required Standard of Proficiency

Signed: ....
(Chief Examiner)

Date: ....

The British Horse Society
Stoneleigh Deer Park
Kenilworth
Warwickshire
CV8 2XZ

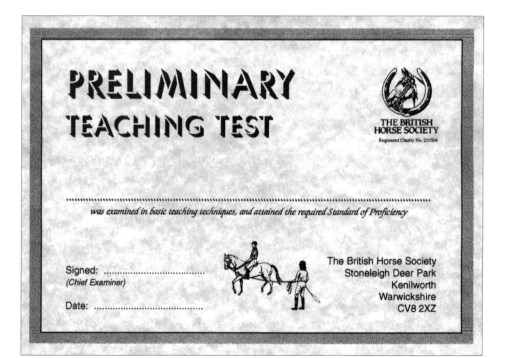

PRELIMINARY
TEACHING TEST

THE BRITISH HORSE SOCIETY
Registered Charity No. 210504

....

was examined in basic teaching techniques, and attained the required Standard of Proficiency

Signed: ....
(Chief Examiner)

Date: ....

The British Horse Society
Stoneleigh Deer Park
Kenilworth
Warwickshire
CV8 2XZ

1. Timetable/Programme for Stage 3

3 examiners including 1 chief
10 riding candidates
12 care candidates

8.00–8.15	Candidates assemble	
8.15	Riding candidates walk jumping courses	
8.30	Candidates' introduction and briefing	
9.00	1 to 5	Riding on the flat
	7 to 12	Practical stable management
10.00	7 to 11	Riding on the flat
	1 to 6	Practical stable management
11.00	BREAK	
11.10	1 to 5	Jump riding
	7 to 12	Theory
12.10	7 to 11	Jump riding
	1 to 6	Theory
1.10	LUNCH	
2.00	1 to 6	Lungeing
	7 to 12	Practical oral
3.10	7 to 12	Lungeing
	1 to 6	Practical oral
4.20	Finish	

2. Timetable/Programme for PTT

8.30	Candidates assemble for briefing	
9.00	1 and 2 3 to 6	Class lesson Written paper
9.15	7 to 12	Theory followed by lectures
9.40	3 and 4	Class lesson
10.20	5 and 6	Class lesson
11.00	7 and 8 9 to 12	Class lesson Written paper
11.15	1 to 6	Theory followed by lectures
11.40	9 and 10	Class lesson
12.20	11 and 12 1, 2, 7 and 8	Class lesson Written paper
1.00	LUNCH	
2.00		Lunge novice adult 6/8 candidates Lead rein lesson for beginner 4/6 candidates
2.00	6 candidates per group	Theory session to cover sports psychology and child protection in sport
2.45	Groups exchange for final session	

3. Suggested Lesson Topics for PTT

1 Assess your riders' ability and teach them to improve their position on the flat using appropriate exercises and movements.

2 Assess your riders' ability and, using appropriate exercises, work to improve their coordination and application of the aids.

3 Assess your riders' ability and work to improve their feel for rhythm and balance using appropriate exercises and movements.

4 Assess your riders' ability and teach them to improve their transition work whilst ensuring their basic position is maintained.

5 Assess your riders' ability over a single fence and then, using several fences, work to improve their position and feel.

6 Assess your riders' ability over a single fence and then work to improve their riding of the approach and getaway using several fences.

7 Assess your riders' ability over ground poles then work to improve their position, coordination and feel for rhythm, both in jumping and upright seat.

8 Assess your riders' ability over a single fence and progress to using a grid of fences to improve the riders' position and feel.

4. Typical Subjects for Five-Minute Talks

1 Care of the horse's feet.

2 Checking a saddle for safety.

3 New Zealand rugs.

4 The importance of a daily routine.

5 Catching horses/ponies up for work and turning out afterwards.

6 Checking fields for safety.

Any simple stable management subject that a PTT might 'teach' a more junior trainee in the yard.

5. Typical Subjects for Written Paper

1 Completing an accident report form.

2 Making a risk assessment of a yard task (e.g. catching horses from a field).

3 Completing a form for a new horse arriving for livery in the yard.

4 Making up a feed plan for a new horse on the yard.

6. Accident Report Form

British Horse Society
Registered Charity No. 210504

Examinations Office, British Horse Society,
Stoneleigh Deer Park, Kenilworth, Warwickshire CV8 2XZ

BHS REGISTERED INSTRUCTOR

Please ensure that this form is completed with as much detail as possible and <u>that it is accurate</u> for legal reasons. Should the person involved in the accident sue you, this form will be produced in court.

All serious accidents must be reported <u>immediately</u> to your insurance broker and to your Local Authority Environmental Health Department (RIDDOR).

Name of person involved: ....

Name of Establishment/Location: ....

Date of Accident: .... Time of Accident: ....

Name of Person Involved: .... Age: ....

Address: ....

....

.... Post Code: ....

****

Establishment/Location:..

Full Name of Proprietor or Owner of premises: ....

Full Name of Instructor/Escort: .... Qualification: ....

Name of Horse / Pony: ....

Sex: .... Age: .... Height: ....

Owner of Horse / Pony: ....

Address: ....

....

....

Instructor's/Escort's Report:

Location of Accident: (e.g. Road / Indoor School / Paddock etc.)

....

How Accident Happened:

A SKETCH PLAN drawn on the back of this form showing position of other horses, people, equipment, gates etc. would be helpful.

How long had the lesson/ ride been in progress? ....

Comments of person involved immediately after incident:

Did the person remount and complete the lesson / ride? YES \ NO

If not, what action was taken?

....

....

....

Was medical assistance offered / accepted / refused?

Was hospital or doctor involved? (If YES - which)?

Instructor's / Escort's signature .... Date: ....

****

NOTE:-   The accident could result in a claim being made against you.

In case the matter goes to Court, please obtain and list below:-

The Names, addresses and telephone numbers of any witness(es) / other people

on ride:- ....

....

....

....

....

....

****

Signature of person completing the form: ....

Please print name: ....

Position held:...

Date: .... Time form completed: ....

Subsequent developments including medical reports, if known:-

SKETCH PLAN (& Continuation)

Please continue on separate sheet if necessary.

g/exams/register/accidentform

7. For Those Aiming at BHSAI

BHS Register of Instructors

Once you have achieved your BHS Stage 2 and PTT you will receive a log book from the Examinations Office in which you should record your hours of teaching experience. When you have achieved 500 hours practical teaching experience (full details of procedure for accumulating hours, including what counts as valid hours, will be sent with the log book) and when you have passed Stage 3 you will receive a British Horse Society Assistant Instructor's Certificate. It would then be wise to apply to be listed on the **BHS Register of Instructors**. Full information can be obtained from the BHS Training Office.

For an annual membership fee Registered Instructors receive insurance cover in their capacity as professional riding teachers. They also receive reduced ticket prices at all the Society's training days and conventions, including concessions for first aid and child protection training days. In addition they receive support and advice from the BHS as the national governing body for professional riding instructors in the UK.

International Trainer's Passport

Once a member of the BHS Register of Instructors the BHSAI can also apply to hold an International Trainer's passport. Issued by the BHS for British instructors but on behalf of the International Group for Equestrian Qualifications, this passport gives the holder recognition of their qualification in all the international countries which are members of the IGEQ (currently over thirty worldwide). Should you ever wish to travel and work abroad in an equestrian capacity this passport will give you valued acceptance of your ability in a foreign country. For further information regarding the International Passport, contact the Training Office at the BHS.